My life is a grateful mystery!
How I came to know God's love for me
is still a matter of wonder.
But when I look for the answer, it is really quite simple.
As a Sister in the Order of St. Francis
I've spent many hours of sitting, relaxing, centering,
pondering God's great love.
Often during those times,
I've expressed my thoughts in writing—writing in various forms
about people
and all I have encountered along life's way.
This book
is a compilation of many of my writings
with my autobiography as a preface to them all.
May you enjoy my works,
discover a bit of wisdom,
and come to know me as a real person
whose struggles and joys
really have been little different than yours.
I've just lived in another time and place.

—*Sr. Kathryn Leahy, OSF*

2007

Sr Kathryn Leahy
07-09-07

God's Brat

▪ A diverse assortment of writings ▪
including my life story

Sr. Kathryn Leahy, OSF
a k a Sr. M. Bartholomew, OSF

Outskirts Press, Inc.
Denver, Colorado

The opinions expressed in this manuscript are solely the opinions of the author and do not represent the opinions or thoughts of the publisher.

God's Brat
A diverse assortment of writings including my life story

V1.0

Outskirts Press
http://www.outskirtspress.com

ISBN-10: 14327-0409-5
ISBN-13: 978-1-4327-0409-4

Library of Congress Control Number: 2007923347

Printed in the United States of America

Dedicated to
all who have contributed
in any way
for this small miracle of surprise—
that I would become
a published author at eighty-eight!

CONTENTS

Foreword I

Since His call when Catherine Elizabeth Leahy was sixteen, God's Brat has been touching the lives of exuberant students, incarcerated women, and disabled oldsters. Sister Kathryn, current spelling, has ever enjoyed writing. Fortunately for us, her stories of the happy, the sad, the sentimental, and the curious are hereby gathered for our reading pleasure.

Hehaka Sapa, or Black Elk, reminds:

> "Everything an Indian does is in a circle because the power of the world works in circles—even the seasons form a great circle and always come back to where they were. Human life is a circle from childhood to childhood; so it is in everything where power moves."

That mystical, awesome power was ever circling in Sister Kathryn Leahy's life, repeatedly sending her back to familiar haunts—even unto her eighty-eighth year which finds her in Alliance, Nebraska, where she taught at St. Agnes Academy in 1941. Relish her shared exuberance bathed in hope and humor and wonder.

— Catherine Lazers Bauer
freelance writer, syndicated columnist & writing instructor
author of *One Day on Earth: A Third Eye View*

FOREWORD II

Dear Readers,

I've just completed a Once-In-A-Lifetime Adventure!! And what an adventure and privilege it has been! Challenging? Definitely!! Exhilarating? Truly!! Enjoyable? Most!!

Now, you hold in your hands your opportunity to enjoy the souvenirs of my Adventure—Sr. Kathryn Leahy's reminiscent life story and her many writings written over the last thirty-some years. Just as I did, I expect you will be able to relate, in some way, to most every thing you read in her book. It's the kind of book that can be digested in small bites, a bit at a time.

Inspiration, consolation, nostalgia, courage, chuckles, perhaps even a few tears, will be with you throughout your reading of *God's Brat.* You will come to know Sr. Kathryn, a k a God's Brat, who, indeed, is a real, still vibrant person who has lived and survived through hard times and good ones. She may have been a brat at one time, but through my time spent with her preparing the manuscript for this book, I've found that no longer to be true. At eighty-eight-years-young, despite wheelchair confinement and hearing impairment, she's still very much a teacher—sharing wisdom, patience, understanding, kindness and the value of prayer.

When I accepted the task of typing about twenty-five pages of Sr. Kathryn's autobiography, little did I know about the person and nothing of her writings. It was only after working with her for about two months, that I finally realized that this was the lady I knew as Sr. Bartholomew, who, nearly a life-time ago, was in charge of the little boys' dormitory at St. Agnes Academy when I was a high school boarding student there. When she was in charge of the little girls' dormitory, my little sister was one of her girls. And so, life not only has come full circle for Sr. Kathryn, but also for me. I reflect on this revelation as kind of a side-trip on my adventure with God's Brat.

Before this, neither Sr. Kathryn or I had knowledge of what self-publishing truly involved. We've hung in together, survived the steep learning curves, and have succeeded in presenting, for your enjoyment, everything within the covers of *God's Brat.*

May you enjoy your adventure into her world as much as I!

—Myrtle "Murt" Letcher,
Author Assistant/Editor

Postscript: Wherever possible, we have noted the date or approximate time frame of each writing and the inspiration for it. Sr. Kathryn says she did not really begin writing until the latter 1970s, so all undated writings have been written since then, we just don't know exactly when or where.

To those of you who have been the recipients of Sr. Kathryn's writings through the years, you may notice that certain stories do not read exactly the way you remember. Well, that's most likely true! You see, once Sister's writings were gathered together and sorted out, it quickly became obvious that she had written on the same topics many times. Each version had the same theme, sometimes even some of the same words, but there were no two exactly alike. It was my task to type each one as written, spread them out side by side, then pull all versions into one composite story for *God's Brat.* This is one big reason why publication time was delayed.

Sr. Kathryn and I have worked as a team to keep her choice of words and her style of writing intact. She has proofed each of her writings, from beginning to end, through all the evolutions necessary to present them here. Nothing has gone into *God's Brat* without her approval.

–ml

ACKNOWLEDGEMENTS

This book came into being through prayer for a volunteer to help me complete a gift for my family—a little booklet containing my life story and some of my writings.

My prayer for a volunteer was answered. But as the project progressed, "Is this all you have, or is there more?" Little did my volunteer know what was to come. Really, neither did I. The search began! My cluttered files contained scraps of paper, partially filled note books, typed originals and copies, and more. As the search continued, it yielded quite an assortment of writings. We prayed for guidance.

Yes, there was a potential book, but was there a desire for it? We spread the word. Pre-publication orders started arriving, along with words of encouragement and monetary assistance. Emphatically, the response was an affirmative, "**Yes!**" And so, with God's guidance and the help of many individuals, *God's Brat* came to be.

Among the many who helped, there are some who deserve special recognition:

Catherine Lazers Bauer, respected author and teacher, who was the first to give me sincere encouragement to write.

Thecla Knickrehm, Vallie Hardy, and all others who contributed financially to defray publication costs.

Each one who responded to my book survey, and all who ordered pre-publication copies, without knowing exactly the content of the book or the retail price.

Tom McCarthy, editor and printer of a small booklet, *Our Mother's*

Dahlias, which contains a few of my *Childhood Memories* stories. His booklet provided the key to begin the search which brought these writings of mine together for this, *God's Brat.*

Family members who searched their photo boxes and albums for family pictures.

Sisters and Staff at Marian Residence for their prayers.

Doreen Wagner and Mary Heumesser for their most generous gifts of time and talent in typing the first draft of my autobiography and church bulletin columns.

Murt Letcher, a Franciscan Associate, for her gift of time, for picking up where Doreen and Mary left off. She it was who found my writings could be a book. And so, Murt extended her commitment and, in addition to typing, became my assistant, editor, and trouble-shooter. It was she who gave this book birth through her relentless encouragement, intense work, and persistent enthusiasm.

Steph's Studio—Steph Mantooth, photographer—who came to Marian Residence for my photo-shoot, and who designed our book's front cover.

Steve and Patricia Nelson, Mary Schadwinkle, Deanna Johnson and Stephanie Amm for proof reading various parts of the manuscript and critique.

The staff at Outskirts Press for their outstanding, professional guidance throughout this, our first self-publishing experience.

1

God's Brat

My Story

God's Brat—Growing Up

Marian Residence, Alliance, Nebraska
2006

Once I was an ornery brat,
Sometimes thin, other times fat.
Time, I found, did not stand still
While I waited for God to fill *my* bill.

Now I'm old and deaf and gray,
But God loves me anyway,
A fact I learned along the way
That made every day a happy day.

To struggle for growth and maturity,
I found t'was only God's love
That could make me real, so
Now I desire only to fill *God's* bill.

☺ ☹ ☺ ☹ ☺ ☹ ☺

October, 2006 ©Steph's Studio

MY STORY

2005 - rev. 2006

Yes, the title is apt. I was a self-willed, stubborn, quick tempered, selfish and proud brat who tried my family's patience. With God's help and the goodness of my family and others, I was able to overcome, to an extent, the force of these bad traits, which will be uprooted only at death. God chose me to do His work in spite of my brattiness. Here is my story:

This event, my birth, as told and re-told to me, goes something like this:

I came into this world in our farm home six miles southeast of Ewing, Nebraska. I was always told I was born on November tenth, 1919, but November eleventh, 1919 is on my birth certificate. Does this give me the right to celebrate twice a year?

It was snowing a good deal on that dark and cold night. When Mom told him it was time, Dad hitched the horses to the buggy and drove over to the Vandersnickt place to get Rose Vandersnickt, a good neighbor and a midwife, to help with my delivery. (It was common in those days to have uncertified midwives help in deliveries when weather made the Doctor's trip to the home impossible.)

Rose also liked to re-tell the story of my birth. So with all their recounting of it, it all seemed very dramatic to me.

On January thirteenth, 1920, I was baptized Catherine Elizabeth Leahy at St. Peter's Catholic Church in Ewing.

Mom also told me that I did not learn to talk until the end of my second year, but I've been making up for it ever since.

My mother was Barbara Bauer Leahy, daughter of Frank and Bibiana Bauer who were German Immigrants. My father was Thomas Leahy who came to Nebraska from Ohio with his two brothers, James and Michael. Their parents were Bartholomew and Ellen Starkey Leahy. Dad was a rancher who rented the farm from Grandpa Bauer and moved the family into the home after my grandparents moved to town. I was the fifth of six children, two boys and four girls: John, Mary, Thecla, Bill, Catherine and Ann.

Jakie Bauer joined our family when he was six years old. The story of his arrival is told about in *Childhood Memories–Family Members.*

My childhood days were centered mostly around home, family, farm life, our rural School District #227, and neighbors. Throughout the past thirty-plus years of my life, I've written both short and long vignettes of those childhood days—stories of the happy, the sad, the sentimental, the curious and more. It is through these numerous vignettes, included in the *Childhood Memories* section of this book, that I share my childhood days with you.

From here, the rest of my story takes up with the first year I attended St. Mary's Academy at O'Neill, Nebraska, twenty-five miles away from home. My need for a change was the culmination of experiences in my life up to that time. It was my junior year. I was only fourteen years old.

I had not been happy in high school at Ewing. One day, at the end of my sophomore year, when I told Mom I was quitting school, she gave no answer, but Teck overheard and told me I was not!! Shortly after, it was decided that I go to St. Mary's. I would board there and come home the last weekend of each month. Teck paid my first small monthly fee from her inheritance from Dad. Mary made my first black suit uniform from a long black skirt and dress found in Mom's trunk. We wore white blouses and a black bow.

Adjustment was hard at first, with lots of new faces. I cried a lot, an emotional release which greatly embarrassed me. Gradually, the homesickness lifted. The Sisters were kind and understanding, and I made many new friends. Sister Dolores, the principal, became a life-long friend and mentor to me.

That first year at St. Mary's, my junior year, was a gift from God and my family. The example of Sisters and students was inspiring as we developed habits of prayer life in a Christian atmosphere.

Religious life had never entered my mind at any time, but, in my Senior year, the thought was given to me by Kate Donason, a Protestant (later Catholic) boarder from western Nebraska. She said, "Kathryn, I think you have a vocation." I laughed! Later, another friend made a similar remark. Then we had a silent retreat, and the thought returned to me. I expressed it to the priest. He said, "Pray about it and talk with Sr. Dolores." About the same time, an inner voice was saying, "You may have a call." After months of prayer and with Sr. Dolores' help, the call was confirmed with, "Yes." No one urged me. I felt it was God calling me to the Franciscan way of life. I have never doubted that call even though, as in any way of life, I was tempted to throw in the towel at times. I have been happy in religious life. I'm very grateful to God for His call.

I graduated from St. Mary's in June, 1936 at age sixteen. Two classmates, Laureen Baumeister and Mildred Wernsman, had also made the decision to go to Stella Niagara, New York, in August of that summer. Preparations were made. The Sisters packed our trunks with clothing, etc.—nun's wear. We laughed at the underwear!! Leaving home would be hard as we knew we could not come home except at a parents' death. These rules were difficult, but later they were changed and I was able to visit Mom before she died.

When my final day at home came, Mom had me kneel down and she gave me a mother's blessing. We both cried. Then Bill drove Mom, Mary, Teck, Ann, Jake and me to St. Mary's, where we waited for railroad passes to take us to the convent at Stella Niagara, New York. Mother Cherubim accompanied us as we boarded the train in our black postulant dresses and little veils. Occasionally, she'd have to pipe down our teen-age chatter. We changed trains in the big city of Chicago. Freddie, the chauffeur, and a Sister from Stella met us in Buffalo, New York, and drove us to the mother house, about twenty minutes away. As we drove, Freddie said, "See, the red roof of Stella!" By this time, I was tired, homesick and thinking, "I'm crazy! This must be a mistake!" It passed.

We arrived and found three other postulants from North Dakota and Washington State. They had no doubt received the railroad passes before we got them. The other twelve newcomers to join us were from Buffalo and Ohio. We were a jolly bunch with Sr. Lidwina, the postulant mistress. The official date of my Entrance as a Candidate is August twenty-third, 1936.

Our schedule began in September with early Mass, breakfast and a class about Religious life or the Bible. Posts were assigned, and we then went to work. I went from sewing room to either the girls' dining room or the boys' dining room where the boarders had their meals. The girls ranged from first to twelfth grade. The boys, who attended the Boys Cadet School, were first through eighth grade.

After that stint, I went to the Cadet dormitory building where we cleaned dormitories and kept beds in order. Mondays, two of us cleaned the cadet uniforms, a job I endured but hated. Tuesday was laundry day for those who could leave their posts. We rubbed hot starch, then cold starch, into the white veiling pieces worn by the Sisters. Other sisters ironed them. When allowed to talk, we'd joke about who invented such a solution to stiffen those pieces. I did wonder about spending so much time to starch veiling when we could be helping people. The thought was never expressed.

One year after entering, we had Reception Day. For us, it was August sixteenth, 1937. My family had raised turkeys and saved money for the trip to Stella Niagara and to Ohio, where Dad's sisters and families lived. (It was a hot summer. They drove in a 1935 Chevie with the windows rolled down.)

The Reception Day was preceded by a retreat and practice sessions for this day. We were brides of Christ and wore wedding gowns with a veil. These were brought down from the attic once a year for this occasion. We carried a crucifix. The procession to the sanctuary before mass was long and solemn. Our group of sixteen then knelt in several rows in the sanctuary. At a certain time during mass, each one individually approached the Bishop, knelt down, and tossed her veil aside, symbolizing our leaving the world and following Christ. The Bishop and a Sister then handed each of us a pack of novice's clothing and we walked to the sacristy where, with the help of Sisters, we changed into our novice habits and white veils. We then returned to the sanctuary, one by one, and knelt near the Bishop. To me he said, "Your name in Religion will be Sr. Bartholomew." Later

I was known as Barty. When each of us had received our new names, we prostrated ourselves on the floor, again to show commitment to Christ, while the *Veni Creator* was sung. It happened that I was the last of our sixteen to go up to get my folded brown habit and white veil. I became very faint and walked wobbly through a heavy fog, thinking, "This surely means I don't belong here." But I did make it to the Bishop, and to the door where a Sister was waiting to dress me as a novice. She said, "Child, you're in a cold sweat," and wiped my face. The ordeal ended, and I was relieved because my family was there watching. It also meant I was to remain.

Later, we had a good family visit. We walked down to the Niagara River, a short distance away. Back at the convent, we sat on the porch and watched the arrival of a storm. Thunder and lightning cracked. Bill said, "Look, Kathryn didn't even budge." In my youth, I had always voiced fear of storms. But, because they were so frequent over the Niagara River, and I felt safe in Stella's huge stone building, my fears vanished. On the third day, my family went on to see Niagara Falls, and then to Ohio to visit our dad's two sisters and their families.

After a strict year of instructions and prayer as novices, we made our first vows and received the black veil in a simple ceremony with the Bishop or his delegate. The date was August seventeenth, 1938. The following day we were given assignments. Sister Carmen Baumeister, who entered with me, and I were assigned to the Normal School in Buffalo for three years. We were to teach, as most everyone did, even though we had no credentials. They were not needed in some states. Nebraska required such and we were to go there later to relieve Sisters who were to return to the Eastern Province. Normal training was a privilege, which I eventually appreciated. It provided a life-time teaching certificate in Nebraska.

The Normal School was located in Buffalo in an old building that was the first Mother House when our Sisters came from Germany to Buffalo. The number of students was small, but the Community of Sisters, mostly of old sisters, numbered about forty. Some of them taught at St. Michael's school in Buffalo. There were many good times in that place. We were poor but jolly. We student Sisters took turns going to the public library every week to get books needed for study. In the winter, Buffalo had a damp cold with snow piled many feet high along the streets—no snow removal in those days. Lake Erie brought the moisture.

Once a week several of us would go to Mt. Carmel on Fly Street to teach catechism to Italian children whose ancestors came from Sicily. Italians from this area are known for their vibrancy. The children were free, lively spirits who were hard to settle down at times. One Easter Sunday everyone turned up in new finery—not expensive, but spring-like in color. During the singing of the *Gloria* at mass, everyone in the full church jumped up and down 'til the *Gloria* was finished. We joined them in their spontaneous joy which showed on their faces and in their singing.

Coming from a Nebraska farm, I was still backward to city life. When answering the phone for the first time at the Convent, I hung up on the caller and went to get the Sister, not knowing I was to keep the phone on hold. The Sister was understanding when I explained that, on the farm, we could hang up on a caller and they'd still be there on return.

One spring day, we were told that Vespers could be recited outside privately and not always in chapel as a Community. As we walked in the greening back yard, we saw a big patch of thriving rhubarb, the source of our daily breakfast fruit. As we went back to study, there were whispers—silence in those days—to tell us to go to the back porch. There we found two sticks of rhubarb crossed and with a sign, "In my day, bread was the staff of life; now it's rhubarb." Word got to dear old Mother Blanche, and Sr. Athanasia, the culprit, was called up to the head table at supper. Mother made it known that she was offended. Sister tried sincerely to insist that she and all of us liked rhubarb and meant no harm. Suppressed giggles came from the tables of the young as we supported the perpetrator and hoped Mother Blanche would understand. We continued to eat rhubarb for the season and canned rhubarb for winter.

Another memory of Normal days is of Sr. Leoba, a retired sister who lived at the convent. She entered Religious life from a wealthy southern family and learned how to work in the convent. Sister was highly intelligent and very kind. Because of a personality change, it was necessary for her to give up teaching. Reading and crafts occupied her time as she became lovably eccentric. We young Sisters enjoyed her stories told in a delightful southern accent. Sister, knowing her condition, said, "It is my Mission to teach patience because of the way I am." One day she asked me to go voting with her in pouring rain. "I must do my civic duty," she said. With umbrella in hand and habit tucked up all around to form a big bulge in the back, and covered with a black cloak, she led, in pouring rain, down a narrow street. Being too young to vote, I watched as Sister did her civic duty. Sister was forever grateful for my companionship on that journey of obligation.

Sisters Gonzaga, Miriam and Liguori were some of our teachers. We learned from all of them, especially in their example of dedication to learning, and more so as model religious with high ideals and deep spiritual values. Mother Gonzaga instilled a love of liturgy and Gregorian chant in us. Sr. Liguori Mason, from England, was the author of the first book on our foundress, Mother Magdalen. We had a good spiritual friendship.

On August fifteenth of both 1939 and 1940, we made a Renewal of Vows.

After graduating from the Normal School in June of 1941, we spent the summer preparing for final vows—sometimes referred to as perpetual vows—on August seventeenth. The ceremony during Mass was simple. We pronounced vows of poverty, chastity and obedience for life, as the Provincial Superior presided. Most of the group were assigned or reassigned to teach in schools in New York and Ohio. Sr. Carmen Baumeister and I were to go to Alliance, Nebraska, to teach at St. Agnes Academy Boarding School. It was arranged that we stop at St. Mary's Academy in O'Neill where our families could visit. All came and Mom was able to stay at the convent at St. Mary's before we took off for Alliance on the Burlington Railroad. I was concerned about my Mother's health but she assured me not to worry. Mother Erica, Marycrest Provincial, arranged for that visit. God bless her!

My first year of teaching was a big, new learning experience for me. Because Sr. Carmen and I came from the Normal School, we were expected to be special teachers somehow. Education in theory is one thing. Practice is another. I loved the kids but was strict in discipline. Talkers got writing punishments. One thing I was proud of was teaching the children to sing *Adoro-te (We Adore You)*, a Latin hymn in Gregorian chant that we had been taught during my novitiate.

Along with teaching third and fourth grade that first year at St. Agnes Academy, I was in charge of the little girls' dormitory. There were a dozen or so girls from ages six through twelve. It was my duty to prepare them for night in the dorm, which included curling hair—not my prime talent! I slept in one of the pink curtained alcoves like theirs. My agenda for the day began with early rising for prayer followed by getting the girls up for seven A.M. mass. Then it was time for breakfast and a day in the classroom. The next year my transfer to the boys dormitory was an easier assignment. No hair to curl! Late nights darning socks or mending clothes were very different tasks. Five years of this was an enjoyable as well as a good learning experience.

My next move was to St. Elizabeth's School and Convent which was in an old part of Denver, Colorado. Here I had over sixty students in grades five and six. There was a large Hispanic population and a number of students came from a new housing project nearby. There were many broken homes and they knew what poverty was. Tuition was one dollar per month for those who could pay. Franciscan Fathers supported the school. There was no hot lunch program at that time but we did manage to serve a half-pint of milk to those who could pay five cents. I recall one benefactor sending five dollars each month for milk for poor children. Many students, after graduating from the eighth grade, went on to St. Joseph High School and others to West High School. Several were awarded Scholarships to Catholic High Schools. For a few, this was the end of their education. I loved the children and families with whom we worked.

Our staff of seven sisters was housed in the convent and a monthly stipend of three hundred dollars was provided for the group. That amount covered our living expenses, including dental care and extras that were needed.

Our Sisters worked hard in teaching there. We attended Mass daily with the children. The children's choir sang at High Mass nearly every day and sang Requiems at funerals. On Saturdays, the teachers would take the bus to Loretto Heights College to earn credits toward a degree. That was a long morning for them. I would go shopping with the superior at the outdoor market for fresh vegetables and meat, and help clean the house. We were happy.

In 1947, the re-opening of St. Mary's Catholic Grade School at Rushville, Nebraska, was a pioneering venture in an rural area. At one time, St. Mary's had been both a grade school and a high school including boarders. During the two years I was there, three teachers (Sr. Agnesine, Sr. Cecelia, and I, Sr. Bartholomew) plus a cook (Sr. Mafalda) lived in quarters above the classrooms. Because of finances, we pulled out old textbooks that had been used many years before. The children were friendly and cooperative, as were the families. What a change it was coming from the big inner-city school to a rural area somewhat similar to where I grew up!

One year a bit of church teaching was added to the Catechism. When Sr. Cecilia asked her second grade class to give an example of a mortal sin, Jeanie Leahy (Knudtson) thoughtfully replied, "Something like tipping over people's toilets on Halloween." Only a Nebraskan could supply such an answer!! Her Uncle Frank's comment about the story was, "It might make a difference if there was someone in it."

In the fall of 1949, it was back to St. Agnes Academy for another two years, and where I faced another new challenge—teaching eighth grade. I learned ratio and proportion and square root as I prepared math class. The students were energetic and enjoyable. Danny Wetzler, from one of those classes, later went on to become a priest. Once again, the boys dormitory was my night task.

It was during this time that I had to complete a thesis for a Master's Degree in Education at Creighton University. You see, education was important in our Community. Previous summers were spent at St. Ambrose College in Davenport, Iowa for a B. A. Degree (1945) and at Creighton University in Omaha, Nebraska, working toward this sought-after Masters Degree. When I finally completed the thesis, Sister Leonita Hager typed it. The thesis was accepted and I received the degree from Creighton in the summer of 1951.

At the beginning of the 1951 fall school term, I was transferred back to St. Elizabeth's in Denver, this time as principal and eighth grade teacher. Circumstances for the students and their families had not changed much.

Our neighboring school was St. Cajetan's, an all Hispanic school. We had good relations except for a yearly spring uprising when the older students of each school would gather in confrontation for no special reason—just spring fever! Officer Hale, who was overseer of the parochial schools, would be on call to watch the situation. Nothing big ever happened.

We started a 4-H club one year and enthusiasm was high. One special project was "Save Water" during a period of rationing. Another was "Clean Up the City." The students gave their best to both projects.

I recall the happiness of the Hispanic parents when one of their mothers was elected president of the PTA. How the attendance swelled at monthly meetings!

During these years at St. Elizabeth's, I made my last visit to see Mom believing it would be my only visit. Mary brought Mom to her home from the nursing home for those three days. It was heart-wrenching to say goodbye. However, by the time Mom died on

February 10, 1954, rules had been changed again, and I was allowed to attend her funeral.

After six years at St. Elizabeth's, I was transferred to Marycrest Mother house as coordinator of our local Community of Sisters. This meant serving our local community and helping to oversee the building of the new Mother House. Marycrest was also the headquarters of our Provincial Minister.

We lived in three buildings at that time. One was for offices and dining room, another for chapel and sleeping rooms. The third building, the first section of the new Mother House, had a library, classrooms and some sleeping rooms. Novices and postulates made up a large part of our community at that time. The Jesuits from Regis offered Mass daily in our chapel and we had yearly retreats.

Mr. Elzie Praff Webster, as unique and lovable as his name, came to us as driver and maintenance man. He was a retired neighbor who offered his help when he saw the Sisters doing the yard work. Hired on the spot, he was a valued caretaker. Later, he was joined by his brother Wayne, also a faithful helper for many years.

One of the toughest things I was asked to do was to teach the novices and postulants some Education courses for which Regis College agreed to give credit. Regis also added that Physical Education could be taught. Some new exercise records took care of that!

My Masters Degree was the deciding factor in the decision for me to teach classes which enabled the young Sisters to work toward a degree. After a couple years, Regis went co-ed and our young Sisters in training were among the first women to attend. What a happy decision! This was in the early 1960s.

When the changes were made and Sisters could drive, Mother Elma, our Provincial Minister, purchased a **big** Volkswagen and away they went to classes at Regis. The young sisters took turns driving, which they enjoyed possibly more than the classes. The Jesuits welcomed the nuns presence, as they toned down the excessive exuberance of the male students and also brought healthy competition.

When the Mother House was completed in 1959, we moved in—all now under one roof. One former residence was converted into a high school for girls. Thirty freshman girls were accepted that first year. The faculty of Sisters was small but adequate. Two years later, a new high school was built. We were moving along at a fast rate.

In February of 1962, I was asked to go to Rome to study at Regina Mundi, a School of Theology for Sisters from different parts of the world. This was a real multi-cultural experience with religious from many different congregations. Our Sr. Cecelia from Indonesia, Sr. Salesia from Germany and I, while living at the generalate, took the bus daily to Regina Mundi for classes in Theology. Every Thursday we had an excursion of some kind, which took us to the catacombs or some early churches—there are over four hundred churches in Rome—the Coliseum, and other places of antiquity. Of course, we saw the Vatican with Michelangelo's Sistine Chapel. St. Peter's Basilica in Rome was visited many times. Each time we found something new besides the Pieta and Berninis' columns around the main altar.

Longer trips were to Assisi—birthplace of St. Francis, Our Lady of Loretto, and Florence—the city known for Medieval art, including Michelangelo's statue of David, and the famous dome of Santa Cruce—a Cathedral completed by Brunellesci, a genius, after several unsuccessful attempts by others over more than a century. It was through the Church that art and learning were preserved through times of destruction. And what a vast amount of Renaissance Art there is!

In the summers of 1962 and 1963, two of us went to Germany to teach classes in Religion to children of our Military families. After these sessions we were taken to our German convents, then on to the Netherlands where we visited the early places of our foundress, Mother Magdalen, and convents of our Dutch Sisters. Dutch Sisters are jolly! Later we returned to Rome.

In 2005, when I wrote my first draft of this autobiography, the world's Catholic Youth were meeting in Cologne, Germany. Just knowing about that event taking place evoked memories of the unbelievably huge, beautiful Cathedral there. Hundreds of stained glass windows had been removed during the War. In 1963, when we visited, they were still in the process of being restored.

Always, when visiting these magnificent places, my thoughts were inspired by God's greatness in gifted human beings who designed and executed such marvels! Looking back on the two and a half years in Rome, I witnessed important events in the church's history—the opening of Vatican Council II, the death of Pope John XXIII and the first blessing of Pope Paul VI. Being in St. Peter's Square with over one hundred thousand others for the last two events were valued experiences.

In June of 1964, three of us Americans returned to the States by way of Ireland where we spent a day seeing the sights of Dublin and the countryside.

St. Francis Mission in South Dakota was my next assignment. There I taught Junior High School students and again had dormitory duty. I learned from the Indian students that white authority is not always right.

In 1965, I was almost back home again at St. Mary's at O'Neill, Nebraska, teaching high school students. Sophomore Religion class was a real challenge. One student scraped his feet long and loudly during a dull religion class. I survived a near total breakdown of pride that year. Still, a memorable experience lingers. One day I asked a class to write down, in two minutes, five headlines they would like to see in the morning paper. Gene Conway's topped them all: "L.B.J. Ranch sold to the Conways!"

One of the big changes in the 1960s was the simplification of head gear. A group of Sisters devised a soft white head piece and collar with a black veil which we wore for a couple of years, and then revised that so that neck and hair were exposed. We did NOT miss the starch!

The third change came when we could choose to remove the habit and veil to wear lay attire. This was not easy. It was simpler to have two or three habits than to find suitable dresses, which we searched for in thrift shops or charity boxes. Such changes were made in accord with other rule changes in the Order to be in tune with the times. Some Sisters kept the habit.

Another change during this time was being able to return to our baptismal names if we requested. I chose to do so. Having been baptized Catherine Elizabeth, I kept that way of spelling my name until I was a freshman in high school. About this time the spelling of Kathryn became popular and I made the change. One teacher wrote, "Make up your mind," when I'd forget and write Catherine. Later when I was received into religious life I requested the name Bartholomew because of a distant, well liked, priest relative by that name. There were also other relatives among the Leahy's who had that name, including my grandfather. When the time came to make the name change, I wrote to the Provincial Minister, asked for the change, and that it be spelled Catherine as I was baptized. Sr. Muriel wrote and said, "The change will be made, but it will be Kathryn because that is on all of your records. And so I continue to be stylish.

Still another change in the 1960s was most welcome for both Sisters and their families. We were allowed to go for regular family visits and other special occasions. These were joy filled times for all of us.

My superiors must have thought I needed another new challenge because in 1967 I was asked to work in the Diocesan School Office in Grand Island, Nebraska. The job description included driving a car. I said, "Never!" The Provincial said, "Learn!" I passed the test on the third try. Education work in the schools of the Diocese was truly a different challenge. Driving a car was a good learning experience for which I am now grateful.

It was during this time in the 1970s that summer courses in Pastoral Work were being offered. I attended one with hope that someday I could do pastoral work. An opportunity came!

Living and teaching in the Black Community of Birmingham, Alabama, for two years, 1972–74, introduced me to beautiful people who shared their rich culture with me as I shared myself with them. I went to Alabama with Sr. Mary Paul Nevins who was teaching in a Black College in Birmingham. In the summer and on Saturdays, I taught remedial reading to students preparing for college. During the week, I visited a nearby hospital daily, looking up patients from our Fairfield area neighborhood. After their dismissal, I visited them in their homes, and we became close friends. The black people taught me so very much in cultural understanding. It was a gift to be accepted by them and to exchange friendship. Several times I substituted in nearly all-black Catholic and public schools. There again, I was on the learning end of a shared experience.

Back in Denver—1974—I was led further into pastoral ministry, which included visiting the sick and elderly, and sometimes caring for them in their homes. There was great emphasis on peace and justice issues at this time, so I joined with other sisters in attending rallies and meetings for oppressed peoples in Nicaragua and El Salvador.

I also welcomed an opportunity to visit women in the Denver County Jail at a suggestion from our Sr. Elizabeth Fuhr. Ten years of this jail ministry was a valuable experience. Weekly visits to the women there were spent in faith sharing and listening. We provided yarn and helped them to learn knitting and crocheting from one another.

Of the many women who came and went during my years in jail ministry, one comes to mind. Marge was an addicted glue sniffer and was an inmate for a few days every few months during my time there. She came to our faith sharing group and was always grateful for the yarn I brought. Marge had a way of finding the bag and getting first choice, which sometimes caused a minor battle with others. When I asked about Marge's future, the supervisors told me she would probably continue to be incarcerated until she was ready for a nursing home. That says much about our need for reform in our penal institutions. Marge once gave me a large crocheted cross which was a grim reminder of the needs of those confined to jails and prisons.

Again, the goodness of humanity revealed itself in good women who failed sometimes in small things due to environment and the system. Those years found me growing in compassion for these women and the elderly in nursing homes where I visited. My sense of justice deepened.

This now brings me to my past twenty-six years of ministry to the elderly. It all began with an interview with Fr. Bill Breslin of St. Mary Magdalene Parish in 1978. They needed a Sister as Minister to the Elderly, whose responsibility included five nursing homes, the homebound of the parish, and, until it's closing, terminal patients in a cancer hospital located in the parish. Quite a challenge it seemed until Father explained I would not be in every nursing home every day. I gave it a try and soon found I could remember names and manage the scheduling of Communion Services in each home every two weeks. The priest offered Mass once a month and, while the elementary school was in operation, each class was scheduled to visit a nursing home at least once—a big learning experience for the children, a huge treat for the elderly who love children. It was a joy to see a bashful child learn to hug an old person. The visits were a blessing to both. I loved this ministry and looked forward to every visit made to a nursing home or home bound person. I liked teaching and my work in education, but I do admit there were some days when I didn't feel upbeat about the day's task

Leading a Communion Service brought me close to these friends in a spiritual relationship. Not all could relate. Groups included disabled and Alzheimer patients. Some knew what Communion was. Others could appreciate a simple homily. From time to time, I would emphasize the importance of their service to God, that their uselessness is their service to God because of their desire to do God's will without doing anything to please one's self—Yes, inactivity **is** a prayer when I offer my uselessness to God. Their faces showed agreement and encouragement when we did this as a group or individually.

In visits, they enjoyed talking about family, cooking and work, among other things. In every person there was a depth of life experience that made for simple to profound wisdom which revealed itself in silence or wise communication. Sometimes it could be gentle gossip about daily affairs. A wise or humorous remark was often off the cuff. A joke told after Communion Service always called forth a good laugh from those who could understand it.

Here I share one joke that was given to me by Jim Quinn, a dear friend, now deceased. It always brought a laugh. Because of failed memories, it was always new:

> Three little mice died and went to heaven. One day God met them and asked, "How do you like it up here?"
>
> "Oh, it's wonderful, but if we had roller skates we could see a lot more," they said.
>
> God's response: "We'll see that you have roller skates." More fun for the mice!
>
> Sometime later a cat came to heaven and God asked the cat one day, "And how do you like it up here?"
>
> Its answer, "Wonderful! The best part of it all is the meals on wheels."

My one regret after so many years with these beautiful people was not keeping a written account of their wise and witty sayings. I've always felt there was more than one potential candidate for office of United States President or other form of leadership, if only age didn't matter!

Inspiration was a gift I took with me every time I left a Nursing home. More than once I witnessed blind Mary's reverent sign of the cross at the Consecration when Mass was offered. She listened for the word. Evelyn could sing *Jesus Loves Me* clearly and entirely. Josephine always brought her pocket change for the collection, even though I assured her, "We're the only church that has no collection." A visiting black lady once called out, "I want the Lamb of God," when Communion was given. There was John who befriended Bessie and walked her to our service.

Once I showed magazine pages of birds and bird houses. As I went around the group, Martha made a reverent sign of the cross as she examined one picture. Looking it up later, I found there was a church birdhouse on that page. Talk about faith! Barney never removed a cross and chain given him. He wore it till the day he died. To see palm crosses and nativity pictures I had brought, hanging on a small bulletin board all year long, was gratifying. The list could go on endlessly!

Still, one more memory must be included here. That is of my involvement as spiritual director with the Legion of Mary and St. Vincent de Paul groups in the parish. We shared prayer and faith experiences in regular meetings. Members of these groups were an inspiration as they gave of themselves to help the needy of the parish and anyone who called for help. They are my treasured friends.

Need I assure you, reader, that twenty-six years of nursing home and home bound ministry was a happy, rewarding experience that brought joy and healing to my life and a strong desire to be more like Jesus as I saw Him in their lives.

Today, in the year 2006, arthritis and a failed hip surgery make it necessary for me to be in a wheelchair. It was time for me to go to our nursing home, Marian Residence, in Alliance, Nebraska, where I am today. (Marian Residence was the nurses residence for St. Joseph School of Nursing until it's closing in 1952. Our sister Ann graduated from St. Joe's.) We oldies are well cared for by good nurses. My day is spent in prayer, both community and private, reading newspapers, magazines and books. I make new greeting cards and recycle others. Writing a seasonal gentle gossip letter to relatives, and friends with a word of cheer and humor gives me gratification. There is time for scrabble and solitaire. I am happy and grateful to God and my Community for the peace and joy I experience, and I want to share this with you, dear reader, as well as a special remembrance in daily prayer—that of my own and that of our Community. I also thank my own family—Thecla, my only living sister, and all my nieces, nephews, relatives and friends who share such love and concern for me now, as in the past. May God bless us and our world with peace and justice and all good! Let's keep hope and a good sense of humor alive!

Editor's Note: You have read that Sister has been known as Catherine and Kathryn. Shortly after her name was changed to Sister Mary Bartholomew, her family and many who knew her started calling her Sr. Bart or Sr. Barty. You will note her various names in the picture captions and throughout this book.

§ § § § § § § § §

Junior
first year at
St. Mary's Academy
O'Neill, Nebraska

Senior
St. Mary's Academy
1936

Senior Class in school uniforms, Fall, 1935
(Kathryn, second row, second from right)
St. Mary's Academy, O'Neill, Nebraska

High School Graduation, June, 1936
(Kathryn, second row, third from right)
St. Mary's Academy, O'Neill, Nebraska

Sister Mary Bartholomew
1936 – Postulant 1937 – Novice 1939 – Professed

Sr. M Bartholomew, second row, second from right
Final Vow Day – August 17, 1941
Stella Niagara, New York

January, 1960 – modified head gear
Early 1960s – a second head gear modification
About 1980 – finally, lay clothing

50th Jubilee
at reception table with brother Bill

60th Jubilee
with Sr. Florence

2

God's Brat

Childhood Memories

October, 2006 © Steph's Studio

In the picture above, you see me in my office area where I now do most of my writing and where I make greeting cards. The wall to your left has two very large windows. A small fish aquarium stands next to the wall between them. It is a cheery place when the sun is shining.

I hope you enjoy reading my *Childhood Memories* as much as I did in writing them. What came forward as I wrote was a sense of pride in our family. In spite of circumstances beyond our control, we overcame, moved forward, and let faith and hope grow through all the ups and downs. No wonder we could all laugh, love and support one another. Our parents and forebears would be proud of our efforts. God has been good.

Childhood Memories
CATHERINE

Story Titles in the order in which they are printed:

A Toddler's Adventure
Deadlines
Ewing's "HOT-el"
Momma, Momma
Robert
Storms
The Monstrance
Robin Eggs
Fire
Shoe Polish
The Blue Coat
The Mop
Shoes
First Grade
Miss Enright
Reading
Spelling
Geography
The Pattern Book
Sick at School
Lizzie Tomjack
The Fall
Miss McCullough
A Captured Moment

Catherine and Ann in front of our house, about 1923

A TODDLER'S ADVENTURE

I'm not sure how all this happened because I only know of it through reports from the family.

At some preschool age, I ventured into the pantry and tried to get a can of syrup off the shelf. The lid came off and the brown syrup spilled over my head and on down. The description I got was "biscuit baby" which pretty much says it all.

With no indoor pump at that time, Mom must have used water from the water bucket, which sat on the washstand, to clean me up. I can just imagine the older kids watching this sticky cleanup. Was I punished? No details on that to recall, but there was a lifetime of teasing to never let me forget about it.

DEADLINES

written at Marian Residence - 2006

If a punishment I received as a child had included a deadline, it would have made one experience much easier for me. The story goes like this:

Our small town church of St. Peter de Alcantara had regular catechism classes on Sundays after mass. Our family lived on a farm six miles from town, and we attended faithfully.

As was his custom, our pastor, Father Alberts, visited the classes taught in various age groups seated in different sections of the small church. This supervisory visit was his way of determining our knowledge of the Baltimore Catechism taught by volunteer women of the parish. This occasional visit began, at times, by Father's taking a pinch of snuff, which we kids found amusing.

On one particular Sunday, I was asked a question, which I could not answer. His stern reply was, "Write it two hundred times," as he went on to the next person. My fear of our pastor was less than holy, and I took his punishment. Family talk on the way home did not go beyond my bad luck. Some were in sympathy. My mother advised me to study harder.

Over the years, I've forgotten just what that question was, but I do know the answer, repeated in pencil, filled many pages of a Big Ben tablet. It kept me busy every day after school. This was when the knowledge of a deadline would have been helpful. I just supposed the following Sunday was **it**. My brothers and sisters said, "He'll forget about it; you don't have to write all that." But they hadn't heard him say, "Write it two hundred times." I trudged on.

Sunday came, and I carried a big roll of tablet paper to church, expecting Father Alberts to meet me at the church with open hands to receive my punishment. Not so! This was repeated for a few Sundays. Today, all these years later, I do not remember if Father Alberts ever saw the big roll of punishment, but I do know a deadline would have been a blessing.

Poor Father Alberts became history for sternness and a variety of punishments, but there was a certain respect for such a style that made us stick to the faith. Of course, most of us welcomed the open windows of Vatican II.

The Bishop's visit for confirmation a year or so later was far less fearsome, even though I stumbled over his question about the successor to the Apostles. His deadline for an answer was, "Now," and it was not intimidating.

The moral of this story could be, for those who must deal out punishments, "Make them reasonable and set a limited deadline."

EWING'S "HOT-el"

My hometown was Ewing, in northeast Nebraska, population five hundred seventeen, according to the sign on the bridge coming into town.

Ewing had a few stores, barber shop, creamery, bank, movie house, pool hall and several churches. The town also had a hotel.

On one trip past this major landmark, when I was about ten, I verbalized the big black letters on the white frame building—H-O-T-E-L. "What's a HOT-el?"

In one voice, the family shouted, "It's a HO-tel," and explained what it meant. I learned there's more than one way to sound an "O."

MOMMA, MOMMA

One time I recall tugging at my Mom's dress while she washed dishes in the aluminum dishpan on top of the table. I wanted some attention but Mom was engrossed in her thoughts, kind of talking to herself, pre-occupation rather than incoherency. This was frustrating to me that Mom would not listen. Later I often wondered what was on her mind.

ROBERT

Robert, you were a bad man! You molested children. I was one of them.

Robert, how could you ever destroy a child's spirit and let her bear the shame and guilt of your selfish, evil act?

How well I remember the hot summer afternoon my Mother took me by the hand and we walked to the milk house by the windmill. She sat on a cream can while I stood next to her. Mom's words to me were, "Robert is a bad man. He will be leaving us." Oh, what shame welled up within me; no regret for his leaving, only an overwhelming silent guilt. And I could not open up and tell my Mother! Robert, you let a child bear the blame.

Robert, you were a bad man! How could you do this to a six-year-old child and cause such intense grief to a Mother who was still grieving the loss of her husband, our Dad, just a few months before. How? How could you do this to our Dad, newly deceased, who trusted you as a reliable farm hand?

Robert, you were a bad man! How could you let a child bear intense suffering over many years?

Robert, you were free of punishment because there were no laws for such, but how could you live with your conscience? You and other Roberts, who have violated the lives of children, must surely bear a just penalty for your evil deeds. Yes, forgiveness came, but only with prayer and a long, painful struggle.

Robert, it would take a book to relate the consequences of your act. Guilt, shame, anger, fear of God and people, a self-image destroyed, even a temptation to suicide in teen-age years—if only I could find an easy way out. These were some of the problems I had to face.

Robert, you made God and the Church a tyrant always out to get me!

Yes, a book could be written but I choose not to say more. God gradually entered my life as a loving Father and the Church became a real Home. All of this, due to the love and care of my family, the Sisters at St. Mary's, a saintly therapist, and others along the way who were patient and caring.

STORMS

Always there was a fear of lightning when a storm would come up. I recall coming home from school one day with Ann when a storm was approaching. We were crossing Nickolite's meadow and came to the barb wire fence. I knew metal was a danger in a storm. I'd hold up the wire first so Ann could get through, then I'd jump through and we'd run.

I recall one summer night, waking up to the smell of burned palm and a lighted candle on Mom's dresser. Mom seemed brave and never afraid of storms as she'd calm our fears. This time I knew it was a bad storm if Mom took such prayerful measures. I think we prayed some Our Father's and Hail Mary's. The storm did pass. I can still recall the smell of the burnt palm and wondering if Mom was really afraid at that time.

As a child, I also feared tornadoes and would have everyone running to the cellar when dark, threatening clouds appeared. This brought a lot of teasing, but that only increased my fears. One time the men came home hurriedly from the hay field because of the clouds, and we all piled into the cellar. That was one time I was not in the lead. It was not a tornado and we all emerged safely.

THE MONSTRANCE

When I was very small, I recall being at Benediction of the Blessed Sacrament. The monstrance used for the service was a mystery to me. When the priest wrapped the veilum around the base of the big shiny vessel, I was sure it was hot and he was protecting his hands from burns. Holding it in his hands, with the base wrapped, the priest would then bless us as he moved the monstrance up, down and side-ways to make the sign of the cross. This, too, was a mystery to me. Somehow I associated heat with hell, so that made the experience an even bigger mystery. Later on I did learn that it was not hot, but the meaning of it all remained a mystery to me until I could just say, "I believe."

ROBIN EGGS

Springtime brought robins to the trees which were plentiful on our farm. There were other birds like meadowlark and killdeers in the meadows and pastures. We took their songs for granted many times although my mother would sometimes call our attention to the beauty of a bird song. Finding a bird nest was always a special thrill.

One spring I knew of a robin's nest high in a tree in the grove north of our house. Even though we were taught never to disturb a nest or touch the eggs, I was secretly determined to reach that nest and get the eggs, for what reason I do not know or understand now. Perhaps I thought I could watch them hatch. Perhaps it was something to do on a dull day, or it could have been an urge to achieve something special. I do recall taking with me on the climb, a small muslin bag with a string opening. It was probably labeled Morton's Salt—in those days, salt came in bags. It was certainly a planned expedition.

Slowly I started up the high, curved tree with many branches. The climb was difficult because of, what seems to me now, long spaces between branches. I did make it to the nest, took out the eggs one by one, and placed them in the bag—probably there were three or four.

Trying to get down was more difficult than going up. Making an effort to protect the eggs in the bag added to a precarious climb down. And there was no one on the ground to catch me.

I made it down, but cannot recall what I did with the eggs. Perhaps Mom found out and scolded me and I blocked this out. My memory fails.

FIRE

One of my childhood phobias was the fear of our house burning down. I recall looking out the window of the District #227 schoolhouse and was sure I saw smoke. Luckily I didn't voice this fear. Later, after many glances homeward, I found out it was only fog.

Another time of such fear was after a Christmas program at the schoolhouse. We were driving home when Mary said, "The house must be on fire," because of the light. John had been at the program in his car, but all agreed that he could not have gotten home first. We were silent till we reached the house and found that John had arrived first—top speed—and had the lamp lit.

SHOE POLISH

When the can of shoe polish ran dry, we were hard put one Sunday morning. Mom said, "Use lard and a little soot from the stove." I did and what a mess! My long, tan stockings were streaked with black, greasy soot marks.

THE BLUE COAT

When I was about ten years old, I was growing out of my blue Sunday coat that had a gray fur collar. I complained to Mom that my arms were too long for the sleeves, otherwise the coat was okay. Mom said it would have to last another winter and she could not make the sleeves longer.

Being stubborn and proud, I knew better! Inside the buttonhole side, there was a strip of extra blue material. I cut a strip and managed to make two small strips for the sleeves. Using a needle and white thread, I sewed the small strips to each cuff.

What a sight! The patched-on cuffs, the white thread, and with my crude child stitching. Whenever I wore the coat, I'd let my arms hang down or behind my back to hide my stubborn stitching. After the fact, Mom pointed out to me how I could have made it neater but the damage was done.

THE MOP

If anyone was more stubborn than Tony, the horse, it was I. Nobody could tell me anything or show me how to do it. I knew it all!

It seems I was asked to mop the linoleum on the kitchen floor one day. I was probably about ten or eleven years old. I got the mop and bucket and went to it.

When I was almost finished, Mary came to inspect. She wanted to show me how to wring out the mop to get rid of the last puddles. This hurt my pride and I got mad. Words followed. Then I took the dripping mop and lifted it to Mary's head.

She withdrew fast, with dirty water dripping down her body. As for me, I was left with small puddles of water on the floor because I couldn't ring out that mop as it needed to be. Yes, I was a stubborn brat!

SHOES

Mom always got us sturdy oxfords from Wunner's General Store. How I envied the dainty patent leather kind we'd see the town kids wear on Sunday. When I was in seventh or eighth grade, we were visiting Gertie, a neighbor. Before I left, she brought out a pair of dainty, pointed shoes with a classy strap over the instep. She asked me to try them on, which I did, squeezing my foot into the narrow shoe. They looked beautiful but felt tight. Pride got the best of me and I said they fit fine. Gertie said I could take them and bring her a dollar and a half sometime. I did not expect the last request.

Well, I took them home, explained matters and Mom said, "Those shoes are too narrow for you," and Teck added, "You're taking those shoes back, the sooner the better!"

I returned the shoes. And, yes, I learned something about making deals.

FIRST GRADE

My first grade teacher was Marie Bazelman (Kallhoff) at District #227. I do not recall the first day, only snatches of those early days. Marie taught phonics. We sounded phonics, spelled phonics, wrote phonics daily and then learned words. First it was er, th, bl—then letters added to them to make words and we wrote some more—rows, columns, pages—in the Red Chief tablet. I soon learned to read and could attack new words with my phonics skill. To this day, I can recite the *Little Red Hen* story because of the repetition of words. She taught phonics so well that I could read a fifth grade book in second grade. Marie often praised me.

MISS ENRIGHT

When I was in second grade, a Miss Enright from O'Neill, Nebraska, taught at District #227 for a few months. She was a lovely lady who had a bit of the big town polish. Few things I recall because of her short stay.

It seems the boys, rowdy and wild, gave her a bad time. Then I heard she was homesick for O'Neill. After all, she was twenty-five or thirty miles from home. She boarded at the Frank Vandersnickt home as I recall.

The one thing I remember best is that she praised me often for my ability to read. I loved new words, the bigger the better. Several times I recall Miss Enright giving me an upper grade book and asking me to read for someone—perhaps my Mother or a visitor, I'm not sure of the audience—but she made me feel good by this recognition and praise. Marie Bazelman's phonics teaching paid off. I could read words with good expression, so others could understand, even though I did not many times.

READING

Yes, I could read well, but understanding what I read was always a struggle. Few helps were given to real thinking and comprehension. I hated history and can still recall the big yellow-tan covered book with pages of print and an occasional small black-and-white picture that was of no interest whatsoever. We'd be assigned to read a few pages and be asked some factual questions at recitation time. I'm not sure the teacher always knew the answers. Tests were dreaded.

When I look back now, I'm sure of the reason why understanding what I read was such a struggle. When I was in the third grade, I spent time in some of the fourth grade classes. When school started the next year, I was put in the fifth grade. Skipping the fourth grade wasn't so great after all.

SPELLING

Spelling was my favorite subject. It came easy for me because of the good phonics teacher I had. I could sound out any new word and had a good memory for words that could not be fully sounded out, like t-h-o-u-g-h-t. I was interested in the town spelling bee and felt I could do well, but town kids frightened me and I had the stupid idea that town kids were better, so I did not compete. This feeling less than town kids was bad. It carried over in other ways and had to be dealt with later in life through realizing that each of us has special gifts, and by not comparing myself to others.

Postscript: 2006 Recently I found a couple of pages listing all my special gifts. They ranged from milking cows and chopping wood to teaching school and speaking my truth in public. That list is being added to in thanksgiving to God for His abundant gifts.

GEOGRAPHY

Geography was a bit more interesting but also far from inspiring. Igloos in Alaska and thatched huts in Africa did challenge the imagination and could make me appreciate my own farm home.

Maps and a globe gave us a mixed up meaning of such terms as latitude and longitude. I was mighty glad not to be living near the equator or walking the sands of the Sahara Desert. We learned they were hot spots.

THE PATTERN BOOK

The teacher's pattern book was a gem in our one-room rural school. It was a thick-paged book full of outline pictures of all kinds—birds, flowers, animals and other things. The teacher would run off copies of the pictures on a hectograph pad for our Friday afternoon art classes. We referred to the copies as drawing and coloring pictures. From years of use, the book had become tattered and soiled. A new one would soon replace it. One spring—probably just before school was to be out for the summer—the teacher offered to give away this tattered pattern book.

There were two of us who wanted it—Jim and I—so it was put to a vote by all the kids in school. Jim must have campaigned like wild because when we were asked to choose, nearly all hands went up for him. I was so stunned that I cannot recall if there were any votes for me at all.

I should have realized that Jim's personality and vigorous campaign led to his success, but, unfortunately, I took it as a personal rejection. It was disappointing not to be able to color and draw with the old book, but the rejection—!! Apparently I was supposed to have known all along that I should not have taken it so personally.

SICK AT SCHOOL

One time in late afternoon, I became sick to my stomach and heaved my lunch onto the floor. Embarrassed? I just sat there. The teacher knew I was feeling better then, and suggested I get the dustpan, scoop up some dirt from outside and dump it on the mess. After school was dismissed, I took the broom and cleaned up my accident. I thought it was cruel that the teacher asked me to do that, but it taught me to ask in time if it should happen again. It never did!

LIZZIE TOMJACK

Lizzie was mother of several Tomjack's who attended District #227 school—Walt, Lucille, Jim, Virginia and Dennis. Jim and I were in the same grade. One time a big box was found on my desk seat with my name on it. Mrs. Tomjack surprised me with sweater and scarf, as I recall. It made me very happy.

THE FALL

We walked to school in good weather. On bad days, or for other reasons, we rode the horse or were driven by car or wagon, depending on the weather.

One day when we were leaving school, Bill and Teck were on the horse and they tried pulling me up as a third one to ride bareback. Somehow I slipped down and fell on the ground. I was hurting, but they finally hoisted me up and we were on our way. Bill tried to gallop the horse to make up for lost time. That made my shoulder hurt badly, so he walked the horse slowly all the way home—about a mile and a half. When we got home, Mom could tell the shoulder was probably broken. Cousins Claud and Agnes Rotherham were visiting Mom, so they drove Mom and me to town to Dr. Briggs office. I recall being laid on a table and a basket like thing was placed over my face that smelled awful. It was ether. I kicked wildly while the folks around held my hands and legs. When I woke up, there was a plaster of Paris cast over my right shoulder that extended down to and around my whole waist. For six weeks or more I endured this straitjacket.

MISS McCULLOUGH

I was twelve when I started as freshman at Ewing High School. Elja McCullough was a longtime teacher there. Miss McCullough taught algebra and math. She was considered a good teacher with an eye for brightness. I was hesitant and fearful that first year. She had a crisp voice and what, to me, was an arrogant attitude.

One day, when announcing our grades after checking a class assignment, I overheard someone say one-hundred percent. I whispered to a neighbor, "I wish I could say that." Miss McCullough overheard and sharply retorted, "Perhaps you could say it if you didn't talk so much." Her voice and face still ring in my mind.

A CAPTURED MOMENT

It was a warm summer day. I was about nine years of age, my sister, Ann, seven. We decided to walk to our neighbors who lived about a half-mile away. We walked through our green back pasture, over the barb wire fence that separated our farms, then over a small wooden bridge, which covered a small stream. When it rained, the stream water could be high. We walked barefoot down the sandy road that led past their barn to their small house with a water pump standing in front.

We never knocked on neighbors' doors. Somehow they were always there, looking through an open door or window, working outside, whatever. We just knew we were welcome.

On this day we saw no one so I felt a bit uncertain. Then Jane, a year older than I, appeared from nowhere. We chatted with her about small things while we kicked up sand with our bare feet.

The moment I best recall about this visit was her mother's approach as we were leaving. She gave us a big, brown, crusty loaf of freshly baked bread that came from her oven. We all enjoyed this special loaf for supper!!

§ § § § § § § § §

Ann, Mom and Catherine

Dickie, Mom, Catherine, Bill
September 14, 1929

Childhood Memories
FAMILY MEMBERS

Story Titles in the order in which they are printed:

Our Family – 1924 or 1925
Left to right: Teckla, John, Dad (Tom), Bill, Mom (Barbara), Mary, Ann (sitting on Mom's lap), Catherine and Dickie, our dog

CHRISTMAS, 1925

written many years ago - rev. 2005, 2006

Three days before Christmas our Nebraska farmhouse was alive with preparations. My sister Ann, four, and I, six, were eagerly awaiting the arrival of our Christmas tree. We were stringing popcorn and sorting decorations that had been stored. One special decoration was a big, red accordion-pleated bell that we pampered. Our older sisters hung it from the living room ceiling. Our mother was in the kitchen baking cookies with the help of Mary, thirteen, and Thecla, eleven. Our brothers Bill, nine, and John, fourteen, were out doing farm chores with the hired man. All of us were awaiting our Dad's return from town with the Christmas tree so we could decorate it. The date was Wednesday, December 23, 1925.

Because of bad weather and snow too deep for the car, Dad had left in the morning with a team of horses hitched to our buggy. Town was six miles away. We expected him home about four-o'clock. As it turned dark, the boys kept looking down the long cottonwood lane to see if he might be coming. It was snowing hard.

Mom was concerned. She called the Weaverling General Store at the east end of Ewing's main street. Mr. Weaverling told her he had seen Tom pass there about four o'clock, he should be home by now.

Sudden joy! The horses and buggy returned and the boys ran out. What a sudden loss of joy! The tree and supplies were in the buggy but not Dad. Our worried Mother called neighbors to raise the alarm. By this time, our mother and all feared the worst.

The search for Dad was hampered by darkness and the snowstorm, which, by now, was howling. It couldn't begin until the next morning. Horseback riders, both neighbors and town people, joined in the search which continued all Christmas Eve Day. On Christmas morning, it was John who found Dad's snow covered, frozen body in a meadow east of the turnoff—in the opposite direction that led to home. It was just over two miles away from home where he was found—frozen, sitting on the ground, with an army blanket around him. He may have had a heart attack but freezing was cause of death.

Oh, what grief!! My memory is that of many people in the house, telephone calls, and clothing collected as we prepared to leave for town where our father's remains would be laid out.

Neighbors and relatives helped Mom with funeral arrangements. Dad's coffin was in the chapel of the old church where Grandpa and Aunt Tress lived in the attached living quarters. Mom cried a lot and Mary said to me, "Go over to Mom and tell her to stop crying." We tried to console one another. Mom took Ann and me in to see Dad in the coffin. It was evening and candles were flickering on top of the coffin. Mom said some words to us about remembering our Dad. It was a very sad time. John, Mary, Teck and Bill were old enough to deeply experience such grief.

At the funeral, Mom wore a black net veil—which covered her eyes—over her black hat. She held Ann and me by the hand in the funeral procession. We all tried to be brave as we sat in the first row at church. After the funeral in our St. Peters Church—which still had a Nativity crib in place—Ann and I were taken to Grandpa's house while all the others went to the cemetery. We had lunch at Grandpa's, then went home to our lonely house. Putting the house in order and doing the chores were a distraction in our grief.

Our mother's faith sustained us as we lived through this loss, as well as the following years, which brought both joys and other hardships. Many Christmases came and went with a tinge of sadness, but every effort was made to make them festive. Joy and humor were kept alive in our home.

Our mother's love and memories of a good father kept us and the farm together. We managed to pay the taxes and keep from mortgaging it—so many farmers lost their farms during those difficult depression years. Our parent's strong Irish-German faith was certainly an example for us. Hopefully our families will continue to live out that faith now and in the future. God is good!

MEMORIES OF DAD

written in segments during the early 1980s - compiled 2006

My memories of my Dad are few, since I was so young when he died, but those few memories are still vivid in my mind, all these many years later.

One of my earliest memories is one day when Mom had Ann and me sitting quietly on chairs while Dad read the *Omaha Bee* before dinner. After a while, Dad was napping a bit. His small, gold rimmed glasses fell from his hand and slipped under the rocker. I didn't want to wake Dad, and besides, we were supposed to be sitting quietly. Looking back, I wonder how those glasses got fixed or replaced with eye doctors many miles away.

I have several memories of Dad driving all of us to town or to church in our open Model T Ford.

I recall Dad going to town and he'd come home with groceries. He'd have a bag of candy in his long overcoat pocket. We kids, especially Ann and I, the little ones, would charge him at the door and go through his coat pockets to seize upon the paper sack that usually held chocolate covered fondant candies—Mounds—which we ate with gusto, I am sure. However, I recall wishing he'd bring colored candies. He did, I am sure, but chocolates were his favorite.

One time Dad took me and Ann to town in the Model T. I remember Mom getting us cleaned up to go with him. We wore clean dresses but were barefoot. Dad took us into a shop for ice cream cones. We came out with big cones, each topped with a jelly bean. The jelly bean fell from mine as we walked across the gravel street, tagging after Dad. A great loss! Also, I recall the hot street and sidewalk on my bare feet. We hopped around to keep from burning up.

When this happened, I'm not sure, but it must have been in the fall before he died. Dad brought me a pair of white flannel mittens with red cuffs, and helped me put them on before going to school one morning. I wondered if they were bought or homemade and hoped they would keep my hands warm. Before I turned six, I recall a few times of visiting school with the older kids, so this was a special day.

I remember going to Mass one Sunday morning in winter. Why Dad did not go that day I do not know. Mom bundled us up, we piled in the wagon and sat on hay with blankets over us. Mom put long stockings on my arms to keep them warm. John drove the team and away we went. I think the Model T would not have made it through the snow.

Another time, with Ann on Mom's lap and me in the back seat, Dad drove the Model T to Orchard for some kind of business. Sometime during this visit, we had lunch in a café. A large woman waitress, with an upward turned arm, carried pats of butter on tiny individual dishes that rested on her broad arm, as she carried something with her other arm. I thought it strange that Dad paid for the meal. We always ate free in homes

One afternoon Mom, a neighbor lady and a couple of us kids were walking outside under the trees. All at once, a dime slipped from my hand into the sand. Mom saw it and said, "Did you get that from Dad's trousers?" Yes, I did, plus a few other coins but, if I recall correctly, I lied about it and said I found it. I don't recall just how, but I'm sure Mom got the facts and made me return the money to his pocket.

I have faint memories of men coming to the house and talking cattle business with our Dad. One time there were three or four in front of the barn talking when Mom called them in for dinner. This meant we kids were to be seen but not heard.

While Dad was still living, I also remember Uncles Jake, Frank, and Gottlieb, and other relatives coming to visit and eat with us. We kids enjoyed having company and hearing the men talk.

MY MOTHER

early 1980s - rev. 2006

My mother, Barbara Bauer Leahy, was a health food fan, an environmentalist, and quiet political activist bound together with a strong faith in God.

Mom knew much about health foods and vitamins. Her sources of information were her parents and neighbors and the *Nebraska Farmer*, a bi-weekly magazine that had a little bit of everything in it. The *Omaha Bee* was another source of information, but the subscription was stopped when my father died.

Mom used her head and knew how to recognize and listen to matters of interest and value. She disliked gossip and would reprimand us if ever she found us rubbering on the country telephone line. She'd say, "That's stealing! You have no right to the conversations of others."

Our mother was great on vegetables, and she discouraged a lot of meat, especially at supper. Her often repeated statement was, "Too much meat will make you see bears," meaning we'd have bad dreams. Mom would be at home with the down with the fat movement of today, although the word cholesterol would be too large for her vocabulary.

How well I remember the day Mom acquired a pressure cooker. It must have been advertised in the *Nebraska Farmer.* It was Depression time but she, somehow, saved enough cash for this precious item which became her pride and joy.

The pressure cooker was a large, round aluminum pot that stood about twelve or fourteen inches high. In it were three triangular pans resting on a round metal platform that was full of holes. Three legs supported the holey platform. That allowed the steam from the water below to saturate the unsalted foods above. The lid was clamped shut with strong hinges. Somewhere there must have been a crack for a little steam to escape because this famous cooker never once exploded. Now the vegetables and meat would retain their vitamins and minerals one-hundred percent! In spite of the healthy foods produced in the cooker, we kids sometimes preferred the frying pan and a little salt.

My mother made her own yogurt by placing a pan of separated milk on top of the warming shelf above the stove. This would set for several hours. Then Mom would get spoons full of the clabbered milk in a saucer, sprinkle it with sugar and cinnamon, and enjoy her delicious treat. Her efforts to get us children to do likewise were seldom successful. One sister recalled an occasion of the family planning a meal for a company, when one child remarked, "Mom will probably want cottage cheese sandwiches."

Spring held a special delight for our mother. Mom loved the outdoors! Every blade of grass, wildflower and bird were held in great respect. The songs of the robin, meadowlark and killdeer were, to her, great gifts from God. She was friend of animals and was angered by any sign of neglect or cruelty. We were encouraged always to be kind to animals. Saint Francis surely loved our mother! Sunrises and sunsets were her specialty. In Nebraska, they were the best and after I left home, she would send me clippings of Nebraska sunsets. I recall one Easter morning when my mother took my little sister and me outside to see the sun dance. We looked through the cottonwood trees swaying in the wind to see the sun dancing and rejoicing that Christ is risen. My mother needed that hope.

Although marches and demonstrations were unheard of, my mother was a peace and justice advocate by example. Voting was a sacred duty for her. One year, when the car wouldn't start on election day, she got a neighbor to take her to the town polls six miles away. Even our rural school board elections were important. She maintained silence when we'd probe, "Who did you vote for?" Mom was all too wise to give names, knowing how quickly minor feuds could develop over such differences.

More than once I heard her conversing with people about World War I and the unjust Treaty of Versailles that followed. She often lamented our country's too rigid Immigration laws saying, "We must share this big country. Then God will bless it."

On one occasion Mom went to court to defend a family in need. Another time she spoke out strongly to a pastor's frequent request for money when all the farmers were hard up.

Our mother's was a thrifty nature. She never ever threw a thing away, but found a use for everything. Rainwater was saved in the copper boiler for washing hair and bleaching clothes. "Necessity is the mother of invention," was one of her favorite sayings.

Mom loved the poor. Although she had little herself, others were considered more in need and came first. What she gave was shared humbly and with love. Several years ago a neighbor told a family member, "Your family would never have had Christmas had it not been for Barbara."

Throughout her life, our mother maintained a pleasant sense of humor. One of the few movies she ever saw had Will Rogers at his best. She always said, "He is just what we need in these times of drought and dust storms."

Mom's strong faith enabled her to pick up and go on when she was widowed at forty-six, and again when she had a stroke four years later.

My mother was ahead of her time. She took the best from the past, lived in the now, as she unquestioningly faced the future with hope. Her's was a strong faith!

If mother were living today, she would be hopeful to see so many people working to make the world a better place. She would not cry over spilt milk, but would look beyond what appears hopeless. I believe she would take for her models, people like Pete Seeger, the peacemaker and environmentalist.

"Think globally and act locally,"
"The world won't be saved until your soul is saved."

ANN LEAHY CRAIN

2006

Ann was always Babe in our family until she became a teenager. She also went to School District #227 with brother Bill, either riding horseback, or walking, depending on the weather.

I recall the red and white polka-dot dress our Aunt Annie made for Ann when she was about five years old. She was as cute as a bug's ear when she wore it.

After leaving District #227 grade school, Ann went to St. Mary's for high school. When I entered the convent, she was happy to receive my treasures which included my class ring.

Later Ann went to our St. Joseph School of Nursing in Alliance, Nebraska. The building, which was their nurses residence then, now is Marian Residence where I now live. After graduating from nurses training, she went to the Navy for two years. Later on, she married Mel Crain who was in the Air Force. Betty, their youngest, was born in Japan. Ann was a good mother who went back to nursing after their children grew up. Nursing homes were her specialty and the elderly loved her.

In later years, visits by the children to her and Mel were a delight—more so when grandchildren joined the family.

Ann died at age eighty. Babe, we still miss you!

"OLD BILL" LEAHY

April, 1990 - rev. 2006

Bill was only seventy-four but his hobby of collecting and restoring old trucks, old tractors, old things earned for him the title Old Bill.

I have just returned from my brother Bill's funeral, an experience hard to put into words. It was a joyous occasion but difficult at the same time. Joy, because his passage meant release from suffering to a new and better life; difficult, because of his loss to family and friends and the memories such a passage evokes.

In a wake service, one of the prayers expressed the hope that nothing of Bill's life be lost, that it would be of benefit to others, that all that he believed in be respected, that everything that made him dear to us would continue to mean so much to us now that he is gone. As prayers were offered, sympathies expressed and family and friends shared memories, there was a renewed recognition of Bill's greatness which was the fruit of adversity accepted and overcome.

At one point a vivid picture crossed my mind and it was shared. It was the memory of a large box arriving at our convent just before Christmas in the mid-fifties. The mystery box, addressed to me, was opened and a beautiful wooden doll bed was revealed. My first reaction was one of surprise and bewilderment. Then an envelope was found. The message inside was in Bill's large scrawl. It read something like this, "When our dad died at Christmas, you were five and I was nine. I remember you and Ann crying and recall saying to you, 'I'm going to make you a doll bed.' Well, I never got it made. After thirty-some years I'm sending this doll bed to you. Maybe you know some poor child who would be happy to have it." Touched? Yes! Tears? Many! Big-hearted Bill kept his promise. In a short time a poor family was located and the mother came to pick up the gift. She was delighted with my brother's belated gift.

This episode was typical of countless others in Bill's life, revealing sensitivity to the needs and feelings of others, especially the unfortunate. His own frustrations and sufferings experienced while coping with his father's loss, assuming responsibility for running a farm at an early age, and being the man of the family, were circumstances that made him real.

Conquering a drinking problem later in life earned for him lasting and deep respect and the love of a faithful wife and children plus many friends. His example of quiet reliance on his Higher Power became his strength. Those who knew him valued the realness of his friendship and counsel. His home had open doors and countless people, young and old, felt it was their home also.

Another incident was brought to mind as I looked at five-year-old Theresa smiling from a large framed picture on the living room wall.

Theresa was the youngest of Bill's eight living children, an angel in the flesh that happily survived a difficult birth. For this reason she was given special love and attention by every member of her family. Of course, this special child returned love in happy, loving ways to everyone. One warm June evening in the early 1960s the town's ice cream wagon could be heard jingling toward the house. Theresa asked for a dime which her dad gave her, and off she ran to the ice cream cart. After receiving the cone, Teresa darted back toward the house and was struck by an oncoming auto. Death was instant. Family grief? Who could fathom it? Heaven had reclaimed its angel who must have now looked with sadness on her bereaved family.

Time and strength from heaven enabled Bill and his family to move on with the same faith and courage that helped them surmount other trials as well. Smiling Theresa, from her picture on the wall, now looks down on her Dad's empty chair, but in reality she is no doubt clasping his hand and showing him the delights of a better world.

Other memories of Old Bill recalled and shared included his love for Doc and Beaut, his favorite workhorses that he could scarcely harness when he had to do farm work at an early age, and Spot, his favorite riding horse. More memories were of his fixing the old Ford and other equipment, trapping muskrats, going to rural school, boxing with his brother, and winter evening laughter provoked by his auctioneering anything in sight.

An amusing recollection was brought to light when someone asked about the folded red bandanna in Bill's hands as he lay in the casket. Simple! Bill's needs were not met in any way by the Kleenex industry. A red or blue bandanna served him throughout his life. It was not an ornament—it's use was practical. Hanging from his back pocket, it was a help awaiting a need.

Bill's need for such a useful item began when he was about twelve in a scary situation which had its humorous side. One summer, on a Sunday evening, Bill, his older brother John and sisters were horsing around in the family Model T with nearby neighbors. Bill was riding on the fender when the car upset on a sandy road. Bill was pinned underneath for a short time with face down. While this accident was taking place, I was at home with my mother and little sister. It was nine or ten o'clock when someone on the country telephone line was ringing the central office. Our mother, sensing something was wrong, listened in, which was a violation of her own rules for our family. (She forbade us to rubber on neighbor's calls and called this stealing other people's business.) But, as she related later, she had a premonition. Sure enough it was a neighbor calling Dr. Briggs about an accident. Bill had inhaled sand when he was pinned beneath the car. The doctor was told he also had pains in his abdomen. Dr. Briggs, in his country style, quickly corrected the caller with, "You mean belly." Our mother related this later to lighten a tense situation. Bill was given treatment for minor injuries but his need for the red Kleenex began at this time and became a habit, so the story goes.

The red kerchief in his hand was a reminder of one companion but another—the rosary entwined about his fingers—spoke about even greater needs fulfilled through faith and prayer. Bill's own family can recount endless tales of fun, facts and forbearance they experienced together over the years.

Was Old Bill without fault? Far from it! He acknowledged weakness and wore no facade to cover it. His many unpretentious friends recognized his genuine friendliness and loved him for it.

In a world that places value on appearance and status, Bill's sincerity and lack of pretense were a great example. His early aspirations were many and he had a creative mind that could have made them a reality. Instead he quietly made stepping stones out of stumbling blocks that came his way in life.

At the funeral service two symbols that best describe Old Bill's life were brought to the altar. One was a rose, the other a plaque with the words,"The greatest thing a father can do for his children is to love their mother." Bill, you did this well as your beloved family and friends testify.

Bill, you got there first—April 1, 1990. We know you've already put a good word in for the rest of us so that we can continue to fight the good fight and win the race.

Goodbye Old Bill. Pray for us until we join you!

THECLA "Teck" LEAHY KNICKREHM

1980s - rev. 2006

Teck was the third oldest in our family. She helped our Mother in taking care of us three younger ones. Teck never liked indoor work. She preferred milking cows and raking hay. During haying time, she was the chief hay-raker. Like Mother, she, too, was ahead of her time for she wore the boys' bib overalls when doing the farm work—we all did. She was good at keeping up the morale of our brothers and hired men. Everyone was happy when Teck was around.

Teck and Mary rode horseback to town for piano lessons from Mrs. Art Spittler. They practiced on a pump organ we had. They gave up lessons when Dad died, but for a few years, Teck thumped out this tune on the pump organ upstairs as we sang:

"I went to the animal fair
The birds and the beasts were there
The monkey he got drunk and climbed the elephant's trunk
The elephant sneezed and fell to his knees
And that was the end of the monk, monk, monk."
–author unknown

After graduating from high school, Teck went to business school in Omaha but returned ill after a few weeks. She was confined to bed for a couple of months. She recovered but did not return to Omaha.

Teck always said her Confirmation Day was the happiest day of her life. I'm sure the Holy Spirit was with her as she helped to keep us on the right path.

I vividly recall her statement: "You are **not** quitting school!" when I told Mom and the family I was quitting.

Teck had many fond admirers before she married Hubert Kinckrehm. They became parents of Mary Kay, an only child.

My memories of visits to Teck and family include her challenging me to read more! Her own favorite books were those of Willa Cather and other authors of pioneer stories. She always brought me up to date on world news and the political background of any candidates at voting time—I could never catch up with her knowledge.

Teck now enjoys Mary Kay's visits with her in an assisted living facility in Wyoming. Teck is now ninety-three, in 2006, and enjoys fairly good health.

MARY LEAHY KAPUSTKA

2006

Mary was the second oldest in our family. At birth she weighed less than three pounds and was kept alive in those early days by reposing in a shoe box placed on the open oven door.

Mary grew strong and lived to be ninety. She was a big help to our Mother when Dad died. Mary took Home Economics in high school and became the family's champion cook and dress maker.

Her devils food cake and lemon pie stand out in my memory. She sewed many clothes for Ann and me. When I went to St. Mary's, she made the black uniform suit and white blouses I wore.

One of the highlights in Mary's life was attending the Chicago World's Fair. At eighteen, she received money left by our Dad and she put some of it to good use for that trip.

Mary married and raised four children. She was widowed while the children were still in school. Deep faith and grit enabled her to pick up and go on. Losing Jerry, a son in his late twenties, was another heart breaking experience for her. Again, faith came to the rescue.

I'll include here a story I wrote in April, 1998 about Mary's car.

MARY'S RED STUDEBAKER

Some years ago my older sister's twenty-year-old Chevy was ready for a replacement. It was not falling apart, but old age symptoms told her it was time to get rid of it.

Buying a new car was out of the question. Her son-in-law came to the rescue and said he'd look for a good secondhand car. After a few weeks he told Mary about a little red two-door Studebaker that had been sitting in someone's garage for years. He looked it over and found the car to be in good shape except for the lining that hung down from the rooftop. The owner said he'd knock off two hundred dollars from the original nine hundred dollars that he asked for. The deal was agreed to and they'd pick up the car after the Chevy found a buyer, if there would be one.

It was not long before a farmer approached Mary and asked if he could drive the old car. He turned on the ignition and liked the sound of the motor. How about five hundred dollars? Wow, thought Mary, as she would not have been surprised if he'd offered five dollars. The farmer wanted the car for his teenage son to drive to school.

Mary is still happy with her little red Studebaker even if it rumbles and wheezes at times. It, too, is showing signs of old age, but Mary claims at her age, eighty-six, it will last the rest of her life. We'll see.

Postscript: 2006 You ask, "Did it last?" Yes, it did.

I will always remember the good visits I had with Mary in her retirement. She loved Willie Nelson's records and we'd always stay up for the late Johnny Carson show. He reminded Mary of our brother John. She enjoyed life and made the best of it.

JOHN LEAHY

2006

My brother John was a happy-go-lucky brother who was the life of the party. He liked people and was well liked by them.

After leaving eighth grade, John did not attend highschool. He had needed prodding, at times, to get his school work done. As I recall hearing my sisters tell, he had a way with teachers. Once he said, "Aw, Teacher, have a heart," when something was asked of him.

John was fourteen when our Dad was taken from us. He and Bill managed the farm, so much of John's early education came the hard way, not from books.

When he got a driver's license, John got a car of his own—a gray roadster as it was called then. It was a two-door, one-seater and what make I don't know, probably Ford. He took us kids for rides and we knew he liked speed. We learned of one occasion when he actually turned clear around on the gravel highway on a drive to town. Just hearing about it scared me to no end, even though there was no damage or injuries. He must have learned because I never heard of another such incident.

John married Rose Kallhoff when he was nineteen. Rose was a lovely, common-sense woman. They struggled away at farming in those drouth and depression years while raising three lovely daughters—Elaine, Shirley and Barbara.

On May 12, 1942 when the farm and cattle were looking good, a tornado struck and they were all killed, except for Shirley, then eight years old. Elaine and Barbara were twelve and six.

CARMIE'S LETTER TO SHIRLEY

The following letter was hand-written to Shirley Leahy in the late 1970s or early 1980s by her Aunt Carmie Leahy, wife of my brother Bill. With Shirley's permission, it is reprinted here. It offers a poignant glimpse into the young adult lives of my brothers. This letter has not been edited—it is worded and punctuated just as written.

Dear Shirley,

Just thought I'd add a few lines of memories to the ones the others are getting together. I knew your mother quite well, as we went to St. John's Church at the same time, but I didn't know your dad all that well before Bill and I got married. But he was almost a daily visitor at the home place where we lived with Grandma Leahy. He would take you girls to school and then come on down there for coffee and to "chat." I can still see him sitting on the "reservoir" of the old kitchen range, whenever he came, especially when the weather was cold. It was a good warm "seat." He was always in good humor, and took things very cheerfully. He always would say, "Aw, Ma!" to Grandma, when she offered advice that he jokingly returned, some way or another. Your parents went through our roads to go to town and usually left you girls with us while they went shopping. In my "younger days", I used to sew a little, making curtains, slip covers, and tried my skill at making little girls dresses and coats. I remember making each of you a couple of dresses with material your mother bought for me to use. I don't know how good they turned out, but you all wore them with pride. At that time we still got flour in the pretty print cloth bags and we made several sets of matching dresses and panties for little girls. But your mother found some pretty yard goods in O'Neill that I made up into dresses for all three of you. I enjoyed sewing then, but now I'm doing good to sew on buttons if they come off!

We used to have lots and lots of snow in the winter months and no one got around too much until it thawed again. It took lots of firewood. Your dad would come down to the home place which set in a huge grove of big trees of all kind. He and Bill and maybe a neighbor or two would work hard to cut trees into big piles of firewood (or stove-wood, as we called it then). It needed to "dry out" for a while before it would burn good, and give out lots of heat. I know they always talked of the "ash trees" being the best. Anyway, there always seemed to be just the "green" wood left over for the Leahy homes after Grandma would so generously tell some unfortunate neighbor to help themselves to the wood piles. She always thought others needed it worse than John's and us! John and Bill would ask her why she gave the best away, and she never made much comment, but knew they would go out and cut down more trees and pile up the wood again. She was always generous to a fault with many neighbors, who came around with a hard luck story they knew she couldn't help but have an answer for. Your dad rode a horse to take you kids to school many times when there was lots of snow, and would take lots of scooping to get cars out. So he and Bill went to town many times and brought supplies and mail out for the neighbors too. Sometimes it took an awfully long time, for the trip, and they were in "pretty happy moods" by the time they got home (after visiting with buddies and friends in the "gathering spots.") Anyway, they enjoyed the trips to town and helped the neighbors by getting their errands done for them. Your Mom would be calling me to see if they were back there yet, and wondering what was taking so long. The days were long when we were snow-bound.

We had just moved out here to Cozad that spring and I felt like we were really far away from family. Anyway, we would make the trip back to Ewing on Friday nite after Bill got off work once in a while. Anyway, this time Sharon was about a year old, and we were in town (Ewing) there, met your parents on Saturday night and we all went out to Summerland. I don't know who was baby-sitting you three girls and Sharon, but we were all having a good time. Then when we were out there, I made the announcement to your Mom and Dad I was pregnant again, and your dad let out a big "cheer" and lifted me up and let me down on the bar, with a "thump" as I was heavier than he thought. Anyway he and your Mom thought that was great news, although I wasn't so gleeful about it myself yet. But that gave the bunch a reason to celebrate, so of course the night was "merry." We all had a fun time and the next day we came back to Cozad. Your folks worried about us getting home safely again, as we always had a car that was just "hanging together," and many times we would have "flats" or some other thing go wrong. Anyway it was usually temporarily fixed with a wire or two. When we got home, I immediately wrote a letter back telling them that we made it OK. At that time we rarely use the long-distance telephone convenience, as it was considered a real extravagance. But a letter took maybe three to four days getting there so I know this was before the better roads were completed between here and Ewing and they weren't even graveled good and ravines and hilly all the way, with deep ditches on the sides and narrow. I'm sure I was a basket case by the time we would get over them, but was always so anxious to go too. Of course, Bill was never afraid to drive over these kinds of roads, but I would have my feet firmly planted on the floor and my hand on the door, holding my breath. To this day I'm a very poor passenger, and I think I am the only one who drives safely. (Grin!) (Grin!)

Anyway, I think that visit to Ewing was the last visit we had with your parents before the tornado. I'm glad it was such a happy time together and we all enjoyed it. Shirley, I hope you had a very nice birthday. Much love to you and your family! Keep up the cheerful attitude you have always had.

Love, Carmie

Postscript: The letter to John and Rose, that Bill and Carmie had arrived home safely, was delivered to a family member *after* the tornado.

SHIRLEY LEAHY SMITH

2006

Shirley was the only survivor in the 1942 tornado that killed her parents, John and Rose Leahy, and her two sisters.

Shirley was loved by both families, but was raised by Sophie and Fred Fritton who gave her a good home. She went to St. Mary's Academy at O'Neill, Nebraska, and later to a Benedictine College from which she graduated. After teaching at a parish school in Denver for a couple of years, Shirley married Ed Smith. They were blessed with eight children, seven boys, and Christy, the only girl. They lived near a Catholic church and school in Denver in a big house with a backyard where Shirley raised roses with the help of her father-in-law. Plants in the house the year around added to the cheer of their big family home.

Today, the Smith children are all married except Mark, a cheerful bachelor and good cook who prepares all the meals for their frequent happy gatherings. They are still a closely knit family. Surely Shirley's family in heaven have brought God's blessing on them!

Shirley is a combination of her Dad's out going personality and her Mom's common sense. In retirement, she manages a small gift shop, where she dispenses not only cards and gifts, but also herself in cheerful sharing.

The following, written by Shirley for their 2005 Christmas Party, conveys her excellence as mother and the closeness of their family.

She also wrote similar poems for each child and grandchild.

'Twas the night before Christmas in the jolly Smith house.
All the creatures were stirring, they scared off the mouse.
The family was born of Lilian and Vin,
son Edward became their next of kin.
Married to Shirley, they sire'd sons seven;
a daughter came too, and then it was heaven.
Bob married Jodi ~ to them came two sons,
Cameron and Alec, our special grandsons.
Mark, our dear Marco, came next in line.
And then there was Eddie who found his sweet Sue;
To them came Jackson, our racing guru.
John wed Michelle ~ the family increased;
Luke and Michael ~ more but not least.
David wed Trish (Heaven's best Angel);
gave us our granddaughters, Tori and Rachel.
Then came our Christy ~ married to Kirk,
gave birth to our Luke and Courtney and Kirk.
Matthew wed Karen ~ and low and behold!
Jordan and Devin came into the fold.
Last came Phillip ~ who to Wendy was wed;
Tyson and Little Mac Leahy, two sons they had bred.
To round off this story ~ the two sides of this clan,
a Smith married Leahy and the Saga began.

JAKE "JAKIE" BAUER

2005

In October of 1932, a big surprise came to our family. We were to welcome six-year-old Jakie Bauer from San Francisco, who arrived alone, by bus, with bag and baggage. His father had died. His mother apparently was ill and unable to care for him. Our mother agreed to take him. His mother stopped writing shortly after his arrival.

Jakie's dad was Jake Snowardt but Jakie went by the name Bauer because Grandma and Grandpa Bauer took Jake Sr. the day his mother died while giving birth to him. Jake Sr. never went back to his family. So, from the start, there was mystery in Jakie's life, but he lived happily.

There was also another Jacob Bauer, my Mother's brother. It was a bit confusing with two Jake Bauer's in the family.

Little Jake was a lovable holy terror on the farm. He loved every animal and chicken. Rural school was a challenge to him and to his teachers but he was loved by all. Later, he went to the Army, then returned to Cozad where Bill and Mary lived. Bill was a very good influence on Jake. He became a successful electrician, married and raised three fine boys. He died at age fifty-one.

His free spirit brought joy to many others in his short life. Jakie's boys have inherited their dad's free, happy spirit. They all have successful and happy families.

GRANDPA BAUER

1980s - rev. 2006

Grandpa Bauer, as I recall, was old, gray-bearded, stern and thrifty. He and Aunt Tress lived in the living quarters of the old white frame church he had purchased from St. Peters after they built the new brick church.

Grandpa's small bedroom was right off the kitchen. During the day he generally sat in his armchair next to the kitchen stove and smoked a pipe. His thrifty nature did not encourage matches for smoking. Instead, he would tightly roll up a page from his German newspaper, lift up the side door of the kitchen range and get a light from the fire within. As we watched this process, there was some doubt on our part that the pipe could be lighted without Grandpa's beard going up in smoke! His enjoyment of this mini addiction far outweighed the inconveniences of lighting up.

Occasionally, he'd used a long curved pipe that nearly rested in his lap. The bowl of that pipe was kind of an ivory color and had pictures on it. He must have brought it from Germany when he came with Grandma and two of his eight children.

Grandpa liked ginger snaps. Aunt Tress, who kept house for Grandpa, would take the round cardboard container from the kitchen cupboard shelf and place some on a saucer for him. While we kids would devour the ginger snaps Aunt Tress gave us, he would be dunking his in coffee. Occasionally, a piece of his dunked snack would land on his gray beard. This added a bit of color to his gray mane.

Every Sunday morning, we'd visit Grandpa and Aunt Tress before we attended Mass in the church next door. Mom would talk with Aunt Tress in English, then switch to German with Grandpa. When he spoke in the German language I always thought Grandpa was peeved about something, but Mom said he was not.

Father Alberts, when he was our pastor, would visit Grandpa sometimes, and they would converse in German for, what seemed to me, a long time. Grandpa was not a churchgoer, but he did contribute his share of money, so we were told. A stained-glass window in St. Peter's Church showed Adam and Eve, with the apple and the snake. It was a beautiful window bearing the names Frank and Bibiana Bauer on a small plaque at the bottom of the window.

Once a year, Aunt Annie would take Grandpa on a tour of his farms, rented from him by some of his eight children. On a designated day, we'd get the machinery in order, close the barn doors, clean up the yard and house, and wait for the Patriarch's arrival. We'd watch for the Model T coupe, with Aunt Annie at the wheel, to come down the lane between the cottonwood trees. When the car stopped in front of the house, Grandpa would step down, with some difficulty and cane in hand, onto the sandy soil. He and our mother would converse in German for a while as we kids looked on or gathered around Aunt Annie. Within a short time the visit was over. Whatever Mom said must have convinced our grandfather that all was well. He climbed into the car and they were off to Uncle John's place. We rejoiced that we passed the test.

AUNT TRESS BAUER

2006

It seems my memories of Aunt Tress are always linked with those of Grandpa Bauer since she cared for him for as long as I can remember.

Aunt Tress was a saintly care-giver and a lovable aunt who never married, though she did have a fond admirer early in her life. Her parents had told her it would not be good to marry because of her handicap. She was born with a small, withered left hand.

Aunt Tress lived with her parents who moved to Ewing after their farm house had burned. Grandpa bought the old frame Catholic Church when a new brick one was built. It was in the living quarters of the old church that Aunt Tress took care of her father after her mother died. There was no electricity. An outdoor pump and an outhouse took care of their needs. When our family made weekly or more often visits, we'd fill up water buckets and carry away any waste collected. We brought cream, milk and eggs to help our Aunt Tress.

Daily she attended mass and took care of the altars in the new church. If we came on a Saturday, we'd collect flowers from the neighbors and would help her decorate the altars for Sunday.

As a small child, I watched Aunt Tress remove her teeth. What a mystery that was to me then. When I tried to imitate, my efforts were a total failure. I soon learned her's were false teeth.

When I stayed with her during my first year in high school, which was after Grandpa had passed away, we attended Mass every morning. Other nieces who had stayed with Aunt Tress when going to high school also did the same. One morning, I recall walking from the church to her home next door. As we stepped through a row of mulberry bushes, two little girls jumped out and yelled, "Old maid, old maid, old maid," and then ran off. I knew that was hurtful to my Aunt. Instead of running after them and clobbering them, I remained silent, which I regret to this day. Such a lack of courage! I do recall giving the bad eye when meeting those two brats later.

Aunt Tress took on an Avon route after Grandpa died, but, being a timid person, she did not make enough rounds. I recall the day two Avon ladies came to take away her job. They were polite but stern. Aunt Tress leaned against the kitchen stove with a look of defeat on her face. I could have cried for her.

When age and health required her to leave the old church, the Sisters in St. Anthony Hospital in O'Neill, Nebraska gave her a room until a new nursing home was built. She could attend mass daily in the hospital chapel. Those two years were happy ones. The sisters and employees loved Aunt Tress. Her 'oft saying was, "No cross, No crown." Today she wears a golden crown.

For any reader who may wonder what happened to her home—the old church—it practically fell apart after a few years. Aunt Tress had turned the lot over to St. Peter's Parish before she died. Later, a young pastor, Fr. Richard Arkfeld, was responsible for building, on the lot, eight government apartments for the elderly of the area. Named *Bauer Apartments*, they are a fitting tribute to our Aunt Tress who lived so frugally. Fr. Arkfeld was a nephew of our Mother Erica Hughes, the first Provincial of our Province, now deceased.

AUNT ANNIE & UNCLE FRANK BAUER

early 1980s

Our Aunt Annie Bauer kept house for Uncle Frank, her brother, who had a bad handicap. They lived in a small house two miles away and had no telephone.

Aunt Annie had a Model T coupe that Uncle Frank took excellent care of. When returning from a drive to town or elsewhere, Aunt Annie would drive the car into their small garage and Uncle Frank would immediately jack up each wheel and place a log under the axle near each wheel to save the tires.

The sides of the small garage were covered with tools, old pieces of machinery, bits and pieces of everything, for use just in case. There was never a sign of junk on the ground of that farm.

Aunt Annie was a good seamstress and often made dresses for me and Ann. These included our first communion dresses. When we were small, they would be out of the same material. Ann's would have a few frills and mine would be plain, which seemed appropriate. I was older. There were usually bloomers to match.

Aunt Annie had this coffee grinder attached to the wall in the kitchen. She no longer used it for coffee beans but it was handy for grinding corn for chicken feed. Her flock of chickens was small but they needed to be fed. More than once my arms were tired from grinding the corn and emptying the small cup of ground corn into a large container. I never complained because I liked to help Aunt Annie.

I'm adding my *"Graping"* story here because she was such an integral part of both my life and the graping adventures. I'm sure all of us kids loved Aunt Annie, but she was very, very special to me.

"GRAPING"

March 19, 1988

About the middle of August each year, our Aunt Annie would take us graping. Because she had no telephone in her house two miles away, the announcement of this important day was made when we met at Mass the previous Sunday.

On the designated day, we'd wait for her Model T coupe to drive up through the cottonwood grove. We'd be dressed in the oldest clothes we could find because of the stains that were inevitable in this project of climbing and picking grapes.

We'd have the gunny sacks and baskets loaded in the wagon. When Aunt Annie arrived, we kids would all pile in and Bill would drive the team to the Beck Eighty at the north-east corner of the farm. It was a piece of lush meadow with a creek and lots of trees that invited lots of wild grape vines to grow among them and cling pretty high-up sometimes. Our Dad bought the eighty acres from a Mr. Beck, hence the name.

The wagon would pass through three wire gates and cross the creek before arriving at the Beck Eighty. This distance was probably no more than half a mile or so. We'd take turns unlocking gates. The team would stop, one of us would jump out, slip the wire off the gate post, pull the barbed wire gate to one side while the team and wagon went through, then close the gate again.

Arriving at the creek, Bill would tie up the team and we'd scatter to find the grape trees. The older kids would tackle the higher vines and, with gunny sack in hand, sometimes climb to the tree top to pick the small clusters. We smaller kids would pick from the ground or, if lucky, sat on a low tree branch to pick the grapes near at hand.

I suppose we worked at this for a couple hours. By the time the bags were picked up and put in the wagon, we could expect to be saturated with wild grape juice which oozed through the burlap. If there was time we'd go around the bend and pick wild plums. The wild plum bushes that bordered the creek were not so high but they had sticky branches. Then we'd head home, scratched and dripping.

Both grapes and plums would be cooked and juice canned for juice or jelly-making during the winter. As for the stained clothing, it was lost for any good use. If stains were few, Mom would use her boiling water remedy by pouring the boiling water over the stain before washing the item. This trick would do as well as any fancy chemical used today.

What made graping a fun day as I recall it? I think it was Aunt Annie's presence. She had a certain enthusiastic, cheerful approach that made it fun. The project was different, happening only once or twice a year. We made a kind of big thing out of it; however, I'm not sure everyone was as enthusiastic as I.

Wild grape jelly was a treat worth working for. The depression era demanded that we use every available resource for survival. Grapes were one.

§ § § § § § § § §

Tom and Barbara Leahy
Our parents wedding picture

1914
Mary, Theckla, Jack, John

June, 1942
Sr. Barty and Shirley Leahy
Shirley's First Communion
one month after the tornado

Mid-1940s
Teck,
Sr. Armella Weibel,
Tress Weibel,
and Sr. Barty

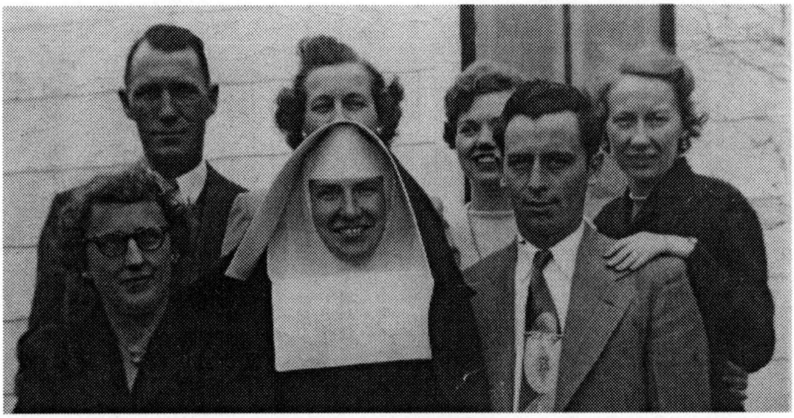

February 14, 1954 after Mom's funeral
Front row – Mary, Sr. Barty, Jakie Bauer
Second row – Bill, Teck, Shirley Leahy, Ann

August 26, 1994
Sr. Kathryn, Mary
Theckla and Ann

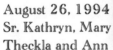

June 25, 1994
Mary, Ann, Sr. Kathryn
at Mary's apartment
Cozad, Nebraska
dressed for a
relative's wedding dance

Childhood Memories
HOME & FARM LIFE

Story Titles in the order in which they are printed:

1939 – Our Family Home from 1915 to 1940

July 21, 1928 – Catherine, Thecla, Ann

OUR HOUSE, OUR HOME

We lived on a farm in the sandhills of northeastern Nebraska. The house I was born in did not change much over the years. It was a white frame building with slanting roof.

We usually came in the kitchen door at the east end of the house. Over the door there was a very small porch with concrete floor. The screen door opened to a small room that had the kitchen stove and work cupboard. There was a pump in the corner that gave us clear, cool water. In the summertime, we'd pump it long and hard in order to have cold water. After we filled the teakettle and stove reservoir with the warm water, the rest would flow into the sink, then on outside through a pipe that fed a small pond in the back where chickens would quench their thirst. In the winter, the pipes below the sink would be wrapped with burlap to prevent freezing.

The room off the small kitchen was the dining room which had chairs around an oilcloth covered table. A bench against the wall behind the table was reserved for the little kids, Ann and me. Sometimes, during thunder storms, our dog Shep would lie under that bench. We could feel his shaking body that trembled with fear as he hid under the bench.

In the winter time the kitchen stove was moved into the dining room, opposite the table, against the north wall. A wood box was next to the stove for cobs and wood. In each corner on the north wall were built-in cupboards. To the left of the stove was a very small one for miscellaneous items. To the right of the stove was a larger cupboard for dishes, pots and pans, and below there was a flour bin and a place for groceries. The floor was linoleum and usually showed wear. In the corner down from the table was the old treadle sewing machine.

Above the doorway leading to the living room was a black and white crucifix. Entering this room, we saw the library table, sofa, and chairs, including Dad's rocking chair. In later years, a big brown framed stove replaced the round heating stove that gave no protection from burns.

A door led to my mother's bedroom, which had a large bed, dresser and her trunk. Holy pictures and a palm branch were found on the walls. The back bedroom, next to Mom's, had two beds, a dresser and closet.

Leading upstairs from the living room was a closed stairway. The boys' room was at the top of the stairs to the right. A smaller room had Dad's old roll-top desk and an old organ we kids pumped and played until it died. A corner room was called the chimney bedroom. In the winter we'd take turns sleeping there because the heat from the chimney kept it cozy.

Our farm house was truly a home although we did not have the conveniences of indoor plumbing or electric lights. I recall when we rejoiced at having a pump installed in the kitchen so we no longer carried water by bucket from the outside pump for household needs.

None of us had seen an ice box although we knew town people had them. We cooled our milk, butter and other things in jars placed in the milk house—a small one-room building situated between the windmill and the cow yard—where we separated the milk. There was a small tank in the milk house through which water flowed from the windmill adjacent to it, then on through another pipe leading to the large water tank outside, where horses and cattle refreshed themselves.

I recall the first radio that came to our house. We listened to Notre Dame ball games and very occasionally there would be opera music. My sister and I would try to out-do the singer with our high, squeaky tones. Our mother loved Ernestine Schuman-Heink, a German opera singer who would be on radio sometimes. Most of the time we listened to John Jensen who sang cowboy songs on station WNAX, Yankton, South Dakota. We'd sing *Bury Me Not on the Lone Prairie* with gusto as we had learned it by heart—one of John Jensen's favorites, I guess.

ROSARY

October and May were Our Blessed Mother's months and daily recitation of the rosary was a must, especially during October. After supper, before the dishes were washed, we'd kneel down in the living room after looking for the rosary to be used by the leader, which was usually our Mother. We'd try to zip through it fast and, when there was a pause by the leader, we knew it meant slow down and pray it right. Sometimes one of us would get the giggles, over some small thing, while draped over a chair. The giggling would be contagious. The leader would temporarily pause with the prayers, then go on, while we kids took turns suppressing our laughter.

It was always the same brother who'd bring other peals of laughter from us during this quiet rosary time. There's a Nebraska saying familiar to those who grew up eating beans. It was, "Beans, beans, the musical fruit." During one rosary session, Bill played his bean symphony totally unplanned and unrehearsed. We got the giggles, but, again, the rosary went on after the giggling stopped.

I'd like to think of this laughter as a kind of farm music.

CREEK

Our segment of Cache Creek was valuable to us. It curved through the cow pasture gracefully and peacefully, providing necessary water for cattle and horses. In dry years, the water was quite shallow, and in places the creek bottom would appear, but always there was water. The creek never stopped flowing.

In the summertime we waded in the shallow water and would look for small snails and clams in the creek sand. It was fun to watch the minnows going to and fro near the creek bank where the water was a little deeper.

Saturday evening in the summer was bathing time. The creek provided the means to clean-and-shine for Saturday night in town. Other times during the week, the creek would welcome us to bathe or just splash and have fun in its warm water. An overhanging tree would provide shade if we chose to splash in the afternoon.

When we wanted something different, we'd break off small pieces of driftwood from an old fallen tree in the creek. The wood was dry and porous so caught fire easily when a match was struck to one end—this piece of smoke-wood was a kind of cigar! Anyone trying this for the first, and maybe for the last time, will recall the heavy drafts of wood smoke that one would inhale, then gasp and cough and sputter as it went through nose and throat. No more smoking?

TOWN NIGHT

Saturday nights were town nights. After milking chores were over, we'd head for the creek for bathing, then home to dress up. We girls of the family headed straight north for our bathing spot, while the men went farther west on the creek for the theirs.

We'd lift the cream can into the car and away we'd go, two miles to the gravel highway, then four miles on the gravel highway into town. The cream can would be left at the creamery, and we'd be off to see Aunt Tress and Grandpa, while he was living, always taking jars of milk, sometimes cream.

Once or more a month was confession night, so on those nights we'd head for the church and line up for our turn to rattle off our sins and later say our penance.

By the time confessions were over, the cream check was ready, and we'd collect it and the empty cream can. The check was for a few dollars, depending on the amount of cream brought in and how high the butterfat tested. Next, we stopped at the grocery store.

Then the car would be parked on Main Street so we could listen to the high school band's free concert and watch the people parade the sidewalks. Fun! An ice cream cone would be a **big** evening treat. Then, home in the Model A (Ford car). Before 1926, it would have been in a Model T (Ford car).

CREAM CHECK

When the cows came fresh in the spring, they brought new hope for that meant a weekly cream check. Any cow that looked as if it could produce milk was put in the milking herd and they kind of stuck together in the pasture and cow yard. Any of us, who were able, helped with milking. Then came the separating. We took turns turning the separator, which was in the milk house between the windmill and the cow yard. The cream was poured into a cream can from the smaller container under the cream spout. On Saturday, or sometimes Wednesday, the can of cream was taken to the creamery where it was tested for butter fat content. Mr. Archer and his helpers at the creamery were responsible for this and for issuing the cream check. Testing took about a half hour or so, depending on the number of farmers bringing cream. The amount of the check was common knowledge for the whole family. It paid for groceries and a few extras, plus gas for the Ford A. Anything left might go for a movie or ice cream. Once in a while, if there were any nickels or dimes left, they'd be divided up among us. Oh, yes, I believe the Sunday church offering came out of that check, too.

XMAS COLLECTION

During the depression, the priest had a hard time getting dollars from his parishioners. At Christmas time every person in each family, including small children, received a small offering envelope with a picture of the Nativity on it. We were encouraged to put our savings in it. After Christmas, the list of donors was read from the pulpit.

When the Leahy family turn came, this is what I recall: Barbara Leahy, one dollar; John, Mary and Thecla Leahy, each twenty-five cents; Bill Leahy, fifteen cents; Kathryn and Ann Leahy, five cents, or was it a dime? My memory dims! When we got home, I recall there was some bitching on the part of us kids for this public humiliation, but our faith filled-mother upheld the pastor, good

Father Vanderlaan, and explained it was necessary for him to do this.

I'm sure other families felt as we did since we all endured the hardships of the depression together.

CELEBRATIONS

2006

Family reunions were always a happy time when I was growing up. They included the Bauer clan to which my mother belonged. The Leahy's were scattered so did not come together.

Special gatherings, usually arranged every few years by our Aunt Annie, brought uncles, aunts, and cousins by the dozen. I recall a couple of these held at our Aunt Tress' home in the old church in Ewing.

When Aunt Lizzie and Uncle Ed Schaller came from Arizona with their family, there would be a special reunion.

Our coming together was a joy-filled time with sharing good food, conversation and laughter. The Bauer-Leahy-Schaller bonds were renewed and faith strengthened as we left with happy memories and any differences forgotten.

As the years passed, special gatherings became fewer and were limited to weddings, funerals and jubilees. On some of these occasions, Fr. Jacob Bauer, son of Uncle Jake and Aunt Mary Bauer of Spalding, would offer mass for the special event. Memories of these gatherings are always pleasant ones.

In remembering Fr. Bauer, I am reminded that our families were proud of the vocations in our clan. We also have Religious Sisters in our clan—Sr. Colette Marie Bauer, OP; Sr. Claradine Bauer, OSF; Sr. Bartholomew Kathryn Leahy, OSF; Sr. Vincent Marie Bauer, OSB; and Sr. Mary Joseph Rotherham, MC, who is a member of Mother Teresa's community.

AUCTIONS

One of our best fun times would be when Bill, growing up and aspiring to be an auctioneer, would practice in the evenings. We'd howl with laughter as he tried to sell some object in the house. It could range from a nail to someone's shoe. One evening he grabbed Mom's false teeth from the jelly glass in the cupboard and proceeded to find a bidder. (Mom wore her teeth only when she went to church or to town.) His description of what false teeth were for and how they were to be worn would have outmatched any TV comedian today. Looking back on such fun nights, I now realize what a special gift Bill's humor was to us.

When Bill reached eighteen, he used the money left to him by our Dad for a course in auctioneering. An ad he found in the *Nebraska Farmer* led him to Indiana for the three week course for which he received a certificate. Later, he received many calls when he added auctioneering to his farm duties.

SNOW SLIDING & "SLEIGH" RIDING

The cellar was the only thing near us that resembled a hill. When it snowed, we'd sit in the scoop shovel and try to coast down the few feet of hill. Unlike skiing today, it took us much less time to get up the hill again for another coast.

We didn't have a fancy sleigh. Instead, the boys would hammer together homemade wooden sleds. None of the nearby hills were very steep, but we'd try sledding down them anyway. Bump! Bump! Bump! Thump!

Sometimes Bill would mount one of the horses and pull a sled full of kids with a throw rope. Once Aunt Annie tied a big sled to the back of her Model T and hauled us all across the meadow!

Yes, we had to make our own fun, but it was fun just the same.

MOTHER'S DAHLIAS

1980s - rev. 2005, 2006

Our mother turned to nature to help sustain her through difficult times, like the tragic loss of her husband, the 1929 crash, the depression, the drought and the sand storms which hit one after another, all while raising her six children alone. Her appreciation of nature came from God's gift of faith which inspired in her an inner sense of beauty.

One warm morning in July, my mother picked a lovely red Dahlia from among the colorful zinnias in our front yard. Zinnias were colorful and grew readily. Morning glories grew easily along the wire fence east of the house and on up the telephone pole on the south side of it, but this Dahlia, a successful experiment, was my mother's pride and joy.

Her Dahlia was placed in a small white vase that morning and it accompanied us to town that afternoon. My little sister and I took turns holding the precious bloom, as our mother proudly showed her prize to a number of friends, who shared her joy in raising a Dahlia in sandy Nebraska soil. A brownie snapshot of Ann and me holding the vase was a treasured memory of that special gift. Whatever became of that snapshot? I do not know, but I remember being happy to be included in the photo. It was honest testimony.

Postscript: 2005 Now, I have more time to reflect and pray. Just recalling my mother's sense of wonder inspires in me a deep sense of gratitude as I have come to value God's gifts of nature through her example. She would call attention to a meadowlark's song, or share a goldenrod picked on one of her walks through the fields.

A woman my mother would admire is Rachel Carson. In her book, *The Sense of Wonder*, this great lover of nature tells of taking her small nephews outdoors at night to watch the blazing planets and stars, a display, she explains, if it appeared once in a lifetime, would bring every person away from their TV's to see such an awesome view. She would lament the loss we experience closing ourselves off from such wonder.

My mother would have agreed wholeheartedly with Rachel. Awareness can be developed as her example proved to me. What inspiration we can find through seeing the beauty in each and every creature, including our brothers and sisters both far and near.

Lord help us to grow our own dahlias and color the world with joyful hope.

DICKIE & SHEP

We had two dogs. Dickie was a small white dog with tan-ish brown spots. He was very playful and when we said, "Dig," Dickie would scratch a hole in the ground until we'd tell him to stop. I can still see Dickie's tongue hanging out and the dirt flying, all to amuse us. Shep was a big, tan collie, also lovable. Storms terrified him and he'd run indoors and hide under the wall bench in the kitchen until the thunder and lightning stopped. He would tremble until the storm was over. Shep was trained to round up the milk cows at milking time. When we told him, "Shep, get the cows," he'd make for the pasture, round them up and they'd come to the milk yard. Shep, wagging his tail, followed behind them.

We also played with new kittens, but it is the dogs I remember best.

MILKING

After supper in the summer time, many an evening of laughter and fun took place in front of the milk house near the cow yard. Our older brothers and sisters would sit on rickety, two-by-four milk stools swapping stories and jokes. These would be about events of the day—hayfield or cornfield experiences, news gleaned from the country telephone line, sometimes gentle gossip from a trip to town, or recollections of our pastor, relatives, neighbors.

Ann and I, the little kids, were expected to help Mom with the dishes before we went to the cow yard. But Mom would often say, "Scrape them and stack them. I'll wash them." This was done hastily so we could beat it to the milk house and join the fun.

When stories faded, it was time to milk the cows, which had been herded into the cow yard by our faithful dog, Shep.

Each one of us had certain cows to milk. When I was little, I was considered to be a good helper by shooing the flies from the cow and the milker with the stinkweed fan, but, when I was about nine or ten, I got my own cow to milk. She was a roan jersey with long, slender teats that no one liked to milk. She was difficult to milk, but somehow, I mastered the art and was proud that I could produce nearly a full bucket of milk from her bag. Not only did the task strengthen my muscles, but it was a big boost for my ego.

Today, I look back on that as a gift that matched my skill to chop wood.

MILKING TIME "FAN"

One of the difficulties of summer time milking was warding off the flies. The cow swished her tail often to do this, but with unpleasant results—a sharp swish on the face, or a deposit of fresh manure that clung wherever it landed.

Every spring the bushy, lavender-flowered stink weeds would spring up in the pasture behind the barn. They stunk!!!

When the cows ate them, the milk had a bitter taste! This would last a week or two until the grass was greener and the cows found better food.

The only good use for a stink weed? We little kids would use one as a fan to shoo the flies away while the big kids milked the cows. We'd brush the cow's back and around her sides and the flies would scatter. The milkers appreciated this even though they had to endure the stink. There was no way to hold the nose!

WIRE GATE

One early morning I was near the cow yard when Bill yelled at me to close the gate. I ran to pick up the post that held the barbed wire gate together. Because the post was in the tangled lines of wire when I tried to get hold of it, I fell down. A barbed wire had caught on my left leg above the knee and blood was gushing out fast.

We were always taught to be careful about rusty metal. So my first reaction to the blood was to cry fearfully and yell, "I'm going to get blood poisoning," all the way to the house. Mom came to meet me and set about nursing the gash in my leg. When the blood finally stopped, she wrapped my leg in a big white linen napkin which she took from her wedding set. Later, when she'd dress the wound, she'd pour hot water on to loosen the bandage. Healing took place without blood poisoning. I cannot recall what happened to the cows that morning, but my scars are reminders of the experience.

BULL

We had this big, mean bull, which we highly respected by staying as far away as possible from him. Before venturing into the pasture on our way to the creek, we'd make sure he was not in sight. One time he was in the cow yard with the milk cows. Ann and I decided to play safe and see if we could get some action out of the monster.

We perched on the fence as we waved a big red handkerchief. We'd heard that bulls don't like red. Nothing happened. The bull remained standing as if he's seen nothing.

TONY

1970s - rev. 2005, 2006

Tony was an old sorrel horse we had on the farm. His razor-sharp back showed how skinny he was. Tony was the horse for the little kids, meaning my sister and me.

If I recall rightly, it was John and Bill, our older brothers, who saved Tony for us. They had charge of the farm after our Dad's death. Their reason for saving Tony was because he was safe. Tony would not hurt a child. He was old and harmless and more stubborn than any mule we had ever heard about.

We'd get on his bony back, for no saddle would fit, and ride to the mailbox a half mile away. Tony would lope along at a snail's pace with head drooping wearily. Occasionally we'd call, "Tony," and his head would lift for a while as he sauntered along the country road.

Once at the mailbox, we'd want to go a little farther. The reins would be pulled to the right, and then the left as we rode down the section line road, but Tony would not budge. Was he too tired, or was he afraid of an oncoming Model T traveling at ten miles an hour? We will never know. We were afraid to kick him in the flanks, a little trick that would bring most any horse to action. Not Tony!

We had a secret fear, however, that he just might wake up and go off with a start, and we were riding bareback! And so we'd settle for the mailbox rides and continue to call Tony stubborn, not realizing that he might have known his own strength and feared dying while he was carrying the little kids.

As time went on Tony became weaker. One day, as I recall, Tony was stretched out in death somewhere in barnyard or pasture, I do not remember which. I'm sure we looked upon his passing as a merciful event. Whether he just lay down and departed, or if the boys shot him out of mercy, is unknown to me. I think we were sad.

Looking back now, I hope Tony got as much enjoyment out of carrying the little kids as we did out of riding him even though we sometimes griped.

§ § § § § § § § §

1920s
Mary, Teck, Mom and Bill at the old cellar where we used to try to sled down hill

1920s
It may be Bill on the horse pulling one of us on the sled. What fun it was!

1931
A family reunion at Aunt Tress' home after a graduation

Childhood Memories
FOODS ON THE FARM

Story Titles in the order in which they are printed:

INTRODUCTION

While growing up as kids, we kept healthy on plain, mostly home grown food. Mom was great on health foods, cooked or steamed but not fried. Potatoes would be cooked with the jacket on year round when our mother prepared meals. While vegetables were cooking, we children were not to remove the lid because the steam would escape, letting valuable vitamins and minerals escape into the air. We must have respected that lid law because we grew up healthy.

Vegetables, brown syrup and molasses, brown sugar, oranges, apples and raisins were provided and encouraged, and we liked them. We also liked oatmeal and cornmeal mush, with raisins sometimes, for breakfast. Sometimes Mom fried slabs of cold mush, which we enjoyed with syrup, for supper. Our Mother's tomato soup was best ever, or was it her homemade noodles in the chicken soup?

Pork, chicken, turkey, wild duck and pheasants when in season, fish from pasture ponds or creeks in summer, provided the protein, as did eggs and milk products. We did not fully appreciate milk products because they were plentiful. We did not eat much beef. The cattle were saved for selling in the fall to tide us through the winter.

Each summer brought the usual garden vegetables and, before the season was over, there were rows of jars in the cellar, all filled with home-canned foods, to provide for the winter months. A big stone jar of sauerkraut sat on the dirt floor.

In late summer we canned peaches and occasionally pears. The baskets from these summer fruits were saved to use when we kids collected dried corn cobs and wood from the big pile for use in the kitchen stove and heater.

August was graping month. The quarts of grape juice and jelly that resulted from this expedition were well worth the hazardous climbs, scratches and grape stains involved in the picking and canning process. Cucumber pickles, beets and sometimes watermelon pickles were made, too.

In early years, the garden was usually behind the barn. We little kids had to do the weeding sometimes and had to be prodded to get this done. I recall a fine batch of melons we raised back there one year. When the ground needed a rest, we put the garden out south in part of the cornfield space.

The drouth years were fierce! I remember one year in particular. In desperation to save the garden, the whole family helped to take to the garden, a small oval tank of water, hauled behind the car in a small wooden trailer. The water splashed up and about as the car jiggled along toward the garden. Thank God there was some water left on our arrival. It was quickly carried by cans and buckets to save the parched vegetables. The yield was poor but we managed to get by.

Medicine was unknown except for the home remedies that cured anything from stomach ache to bee sting—soda, salt, vinegar, onion. Aspirin was considered addictive and the presence of one somehow meant that something was very wrong.

ASPARAGUS

Asparagus grew wild in the cottonwood grove planted by our grandparents, to the east of the house. In the spring, we kids loved to cut this tall, skinny spring favorite. It was a kind of search and find game. If the asparagus shoots were lucky enough to grow up through the soil fertilized by roaming cattle, they would be short and plump.

Mom would cut the asparagus into pieces and cook them with a milk sauce to make the limited yield go farther for all of us. Asparagus was a special spring treat.

BEANS

Beans were part of our diet as we grew up and we liked them. They grew on vines in the open field. In the fall, the men would pull up the vines and place them in the wagon. When the leaves were dry, the white navy beans, as we called them, would just drop off the vines. They'd be scooped up and put in sacks—dirt, pebbles and all.

To prepare for eating, we'd get a pan of beans, spread them out on a table and begin sorting, removing bad ones, pebbles and leaves.

After a washing process, they were soaked in a kettle overnight. This helped remove the gas which perpetuated the ongoing jokes about the musical beans.

We liked them baked, cooked with meat bone, or in a soup. Mom was a health food believer and knew the value of protein found in beans—one of the reasons we grew up healthy!

CHOKECHERRIES

South of the house was a big clump of chokecherry bushes. Each spring the fragrant blossoms would fill the air. In May, we'd pick some blossoms and put them in fruit jars for the Mary Altar which we created by placing an old lace curtain on Mom's flat-top trunk. Then the statue of Mary, taken from Mom's dresser, was placed on the lace cloth. Chokecherry blossoms surrounded.

When the bushes ripened in late July and August, the chokecherries were picked and made into juice for jelly.

CORN

Corn was the staff-of-life in our day. It not only fed the livestock, but it provided many a healthy meal for us. It was hard to raise during the drouth years but there was hardly a year without a yield of some measure. The exception was the year hail stripped our field and the neighbors, too. We didn't raise sweet corn, only field corn

Irrigation was unheard of in our day. God provided what moisture was needed to make the crops grow. As the corn grew, it had to be cultivated. Sometimes we'd all go out to hoe the cockleburs that grew near the corn and stunted its growth. The burrs and weeds were thirsty too.

In late July or August the field corn would be ready for eating. What a treat! Corn on the cob! Then it was canning time. We'd take gunnysacks and fill them after pulling the husks down a bit to find the ears with ripe, full kernels.

The fruit jars were brought out, washed and scalded, then filled with the corn we had cut from the ears. This was sometimes done outside. Then jars were placed in the copper boiler on boards placed on its bottom. Water was placed in the boiler up to the fruit jar rims. After salt was placed on top of the corn in each jar, the rubber was put on and lid placed on loosely. After boiling for three hours, each jar was lifted out and the lid screwed on tightly. This process was called cold packing. I could never figure out where it got its name because of the heat involved, except that the corn was placed in jars cold.

EGGS

It was Ann's and my task to gather eggs after school. It was springtime and the hens were laying better than usual. We'd go from hen house to barn, where the hens had their favorite laying places in an empty feed box, or elsewhere. This particular day I had quite a few eggs in the kettle and was walking south on the east side of the barn, when either a bull or a steer was approaching from the west side. We met at the corner. I yelled, dropped the eggs, and ran like wild to the house, not realizing the critter was as frightened as I and moved in the opposite direction.

FUDGE

We liked fudge and were allowed to make it occasionally, if there was enough white sugar in the house. Mom would say, "White sugar causes tooth decay!"

And so, a special treat for all of us was homemade fudge. In the wintertime we made it more often, sometimes with popcorn too. We took turns, but Mary was the best fudge maker.

The best fudge dish was Mom's wedding set platter, a large, deep platter with pink flowers, which was about the only piece left from the wedding set besides the sugar and creamer. It was used to serve the turkey or meat on special occasions.

One time our brother John had driven Mom to town. That was a good time to make fudge because she'd often say, "Too much sugar is not good for you," and would discourage the fudge. Whoever made the fudge that time, cooked it too long and it was very hard. While cutting the stuff, the platter got broken—our Mother's wedding set platter!! It seems we all groaned and said something like, "Mom's wedding platter!!" We were sad that we had to break the news when she got home.

Mom did not fall apart. I don't remember exactly what she said but it was something like, "Accidents will happen," or, "Worse things can happen."

Sometimes we made taffy. We had a lot of fun pulling the taffy to make it blonde.

GREENS

In Spring, before the garden lettuce was ready, Mom would collect small, tender dandelion greens and serve them with vinegar. Sometimes the dandelions were cooked like spinach.

Lamb's quarter, also known as pig weed, was another spring favorite. Like dandelion greens, the shoots were tender and nourishing, and were also cooked like spinach with vinegar added. "They are rich in iron," Mom would say.

HONEY

There were four beehives just south of the house that were managed by Mr. Primus, the bee man. He'd take care of gathering the honey in late summer. Mom would place the honeycombs in a large dishpan on top of the stove to warm and drain the honey before putting it in jars. I remember one time the boys found, in a tree, big chunks of honeycomb which they brought home and Mom drained them for use on our bread.

After Mr. Primus died, there was no one to get the honey from the hives. So, Bill, our brave one as ususal, volunteered to rob the bees. Teck and Mary helped him get covered with long sleeves and a head shield made up from an old screen that was meant to cover the head. Off he went to the hives. Somehow, a bee, or was it more than one, found an opening in the screen. Bill knew the "bee was in his bonnet" and ran to the horse tank and splashed water like mad. We kids followed and watched. Mary found her camera in time to take a picture of Bill fighting the bee, with his arms waving and water splashing. I don't remember if he even got the task done, but we had many good laughs about this.

Was that the year we gave up the hives? Or did they just fall apart?

ICE CREAMS

One summer in the late 1920s, we had a severe hailstorm that wiped out everything. The tall corn became shriveled, straggling stumps in a short time. The garden, our security for the winter, went the same way. The hail piled high, especially at the edge of the barn and house where it rolled off the roof. Someone, possibly Bill, suggested optimistically, "Let's make ice cream." I recall helping scoop up the hail into buckets. I fail to recall if the ice cream ever got made.

Once in a while in the winter, when it snowed, we'd get a big bowl of the white stuff and mix it with a little sugar and cream. It melted fast but had a faint resemblance to the real stuff. It was a sweet treat.

On Sunday, after mass, sometimes we would buy a fifty-pound hunk of ice from the ice man, Mr. Gunter, who had an ice house north of town. His truck was parked on main street and was fortified with straw and canvas to keep the big chunks of ice from melting. We'd have gunny sacks in the trunk of the old Model A car to wrap the fifty-pounder so there would be enough to pound into small pieces and fill the ice cream freezer. My older sisters would stir up the delicious mixture and we'd all take turns at the handle of the freezer. I can still see the small stream of water flowing from the hole in the side of the wooden freezer after salt was sprinkled between layers of ice. Oh, the thrill we got when the dasher was removed and we'd all take turns licking the vanilla delicacy from the wooden paddles of the freezing machine!

POPCORN

We bought popcorn at the grocery store and had popped corn nearly every evening in the winter. In later years, we tried planting popcorn in the sandy soil. It was small stuff and produced more old maids than popcorn.

My earliest recollection of popcorn was stringing it on that fateful day our Dad went to town to get a Christmas tree.

POTATOES

New potatoes in July were as welcome as the first day of Spring! They'd be cooked with the jacket on when our mother prepared meals.

Some years potato bugs plagued the struggling potato vines. Pesticides were unheard of, and besides, we could not have bought any even if they existed.

It was a hot, dry summer and the potato vines in the east garden were not doing well. The bugs were devouring the leaves and vines. The task of getting rid of these beasties was given to Ann and me. We were about eight and ten.

Our exterminator consisted of child, can of kerosene and a stick. We'd go down the rows and shake the beetles into the kerosene can where they met their doom.

One time I cheated. It must have been a hundred degrees. The sandy soil was so hot under my bare feet that I could scarcely stand to shake the bugs into the can. I found a quick solution. If the sand was that hot, the bugs would die of heat, so I thought, so I hastily made the row of potatoes swinging the stick and knocking the beetles into the hot sand. I did not return to see if they died or not. Of course this lazy trick was kept a secret. We probably had small size potatoes to eat that winter. This I do not recall.

SARDINES

Back in the 1920s, sardines came in large, oval shaped cans. They were packed in either tomato or mustard sauce. On sale, they were sometimes nine cents a can. Has this kind of sardine become extinct? I wonder if they can be found on grocery shelves today.

SAUERKRAUT

Usually our garden yielded a lot of cabbage which we enjoyed as coleslaw or cooked plain. In the fall, or probably August, it came time for making sauerkraut. The ten-gallon crock jar was brought to the kitchen from the cellar and scrubbed for the occasion. The cabbage cutter, a long board with blades in the middle, was placed over the empty jar and the cutting would begin. We took turns pushing each head of cabbage over the blades and the shredded cabbage would fall into the jar below. From time to time we'd stop to salt the shredded cabbage and pack it firmly with the churn paddle or a wooden board. When the jar was filled, a heavy brick or stone would be placed on top for weight.

I don't recall how we got the jar to the cellar for curing or souring, but the men must have been able to lift that heavy crock and get it there somehow. It seemed huge to me. Perhaps we made it in the cellar sometimes, that I don't recall.

By the time the jar was filled, we were sick of seeing cabbage, but we also looked forward to eating it during the winter months. Sometimes we liked eating it cold.

One thing for sure, after leaving the farm, I never again tasted the kind of sauerkraut we produced. It was real! Since then, it has always tasted artificial to me.

§ § § § § § § § §

Childhood Memories
COMMUNITY

Story Titles in the order in which they are printed:

About 1924 – District #227 School, Ewing, Nebraska
Lucille Tomjack, Catherine Leahy, Marie Vandersnickt, Jimmie Tomjack, Bill Snowardt. Note the double outhouse in the background with both doors open.

OUR RURAL SCHOOL

Our rural school was located about a mile from our farm home. To be exact, it was a mile if we cut across a neighbor's farm by walking and crossing barbed wire fences. If we rode a horse or got a ride by car or wagon, it was one and one-half miles. We called this going down the section line.

The school house was a one room, white frame building that had a small entrance, coat room and a flat, concrete slab or step just below the one entrance door. The building was situated on a corner plot at the intersection of the county line and a dirt road. The plot was about one-fourth acre in size. A small red horse barn was in one corner, and two white outhouses were in the back, distinctly labeled. Girls. Boys. The school building itself faced south, toward the front of the property. The school district was #227.

There was a large grove of trees across the road to the south, but there were few trees on the playground itself. On at least one Arbor Day we planted a small tree. I recall the spade, a bucket of water, and kids standing round, and thinking it strange that we have a little ceremony for tree planting when we grew up in the midst of trees.

There were weeds and wild grass, plus plenty of sand burrs on the grounds. The front yard of the school house, where we played games and lined up when the bell rang, was quite sandy and pebbly as we'd know if we fell and skinned our knees. In the back, during recess, we'd play games, have races and pick out friends to play with. In spring, there'd be a small baseball diamond. Boys and girls played together as they cheered for the Hawks or the Eagles, what ever they chose for team names. There was a merry-go-round that was a favorite. We'd take turns pushing, and woe to the one who tried to escape his or her turn. Recess times were usually fun times, but there were occasional fights.

When the bell rang for the lineup at the end of recess, some kids would make for the pump to get a drink before lining up. The rule was, "Get your drink and go to the outhouse **during** recess time." We were allowed to leave the room if necessary, to heed the call of nature, but only after raising our hand and asking, "May I leave the room?" Long stays were discouraged.

Those who rode a horse to school would remove bridle, and saddle, if there was one, place a halter on the horse's head, and tie the horse in one of the two stalls in the barn. There he would remain until school was out for the day. There was a place for some feed to be left for the horse to eat during his wait. Once school was out, it was time to saddle-up again for the ride home.

The pump in front of the schoolhouse supplied water for the drinking water bucket, which sat on a table in a corner of the coat room. We took turns filling it each day. Later, a big crock jar, called an urn, replaced the bucket. A couple of tin cups hung on nails above. No ice or paper cups! One or two tin cups served all. No germs in those days?

Inside the schoolhouse, one passed the teacher's desk which was in the right-hand corner. Children's desks were the old-fashioned singles and doubles, nailed to board runners that kept them in place. The singles were in one row, along each wall near the windows. The doubles were in the middle, behind the stove in the back. The good girls usually sat in the double desks as they could be trusted not to talk. There were about seven or eight desks ranging from small to large on window sides. In front of the room were one or two double seats where we would be called for our class.

Whispering was the big discipline problem in a one room school. The teacher's punishment was writing something after school or staying in at recess. Boys were usually the guilty ones.

The desks were reddish brown in color and each had an ink well. Ink use started in fourth grade? We all hoped for a desk that would not be carved with initials, so we could write smoothly on our Big Ben tablet paper. The shelf under the desk top had space for our few books and a tablet. If one was lucky, he or she might have a pencil or crayon case to keep things from rattling around or being lost.

At the front, there were slate blackboards, one on either side of the front door leading from the coat room. The narrow shelf at the bottom of the slate held chalk and an eraser. If we were prepared, we enjoyed going to the board to work arithmetic problems. Sometimes we could practice spelling words. We took turns cleaning erasers after school. That meant clapping them together outside. The chalk would fly and our hands would become chapped. Helping the teacher in this way was worth any discomfort.

Teachers were young women out of high school who had a Normal Training course in high school. They usually boarded with a farm family from the district and received a salary ranging from twenty to thirty dollars per month during 1920s and 1930s. The teacher was hired by the local school board superintendent and one or two helpers.

Good teachers could manage the different ages and classes well and kids learned. That was not always the case, though. Most seemed weak in grammar. We never did learn to diagram correctly.

Teachers also had to deal with emergencies. I remember one time when a little girl broke her arm on the playground during recess time. She had fallen off the merry-go-round. Our teacher quickly tore off the stiff back of a Geography book, folded it and put the arm in it while her brother ran home to get the family to take her to the doctor.

They, too, knew what the depression struggle was. I recall now a teacher who seldom smiled and who learned many lessons along with us. During winter, she often wore a navy blue serge dress with white collar. The front hem was held in place by a shingle nail. Even safety pins were scarce during the Depression! They were probably five cents a pack in those days but the five cents was needed elsewhere.

Usually our teachers were changed from year to year. Occasionally we'd have one for a two or three year period. Names I recall are Loretta Enright, Marie Bazelman (Kallhoff), Isabelle Koenig (Thoendal), Matilda "Til" Bauer (Rotherham), Theresa Hemenway and James Rotherham. My sister, Thecla, recalled Anna Primus who stayed with our family when Thecla was small. She slept with Anna who prayed with her after going to bed. She was a special teacher.

There were usually about twenty children who came, ranging from first grade to and including the eighth grade, with usually two or more children from each family. The names I remember are Bauer, Vandersnickt, Tomjack, Snowardt, Kallhoff, Bollwitt, Rotherham, Nickolite and, of course, Leahy.

In the morning, when it was time for school to begin, the teacher rang a handbell as our signal to come in from before-school play. We'd all line up according to grade, boys in one line, girls in another. At another signal from the teacher, we'd march in, stand next to our desks, and when all were in, we'd salute the flag and then be seated. Sometimes we sang a song, or the teacher read a short story or poem before classes began.

For each class, the teacher would call out the grade and the subject, like, "First grade arithmetic," and we'd file to the bench at the front of the room where we recited answers to homework. I think recitation time would be about ten minutes. It seems that arithmetic and reading were morning subjects. In the afternoon there would be geography, spelling and grammar. Civics and hygiene were once or twice a week classes.

Our lessons were mostly question and answer. There were few visual aids or other teaching devices. I do recall seeing the black and white Palmer penmanship alphabet cards above the blackboards at the front of the room. I recall my first grade teacher teaching phonics. There was drill after drill of the ch, sh, tw and dozens of other sounds over and over. Then we'd write the sounds, one row after the other. History and geography books were dull with a few black and white illustrations. The geography books did have a few colored pictures but they were dull and faded, as I now recall.

Every Friday afternoon was art day. The teacher had a big, thick drawing book that contained many outline pictures. The outline pictures we colored were taken off on an old hectograph gelatine frame that gave the picture purple lines.

We'd often get a picture of a bird, flower or some object to color. It was the rule to stay within the lines. We tried our hardest with our limited number of crayons which were often broken after much use. The colored pictures would be placed along the chalk board. How they stuck, I cannot recall. Those were days when scotch tape and plastic holders had not yet been invented.

Hectograph? According to one dictionary, it is "a duplicating device by which written or typed matter is transferred to a gylcerin-coated sheet of gelatin, from which many copies can be taken." I recall ours as a shallow, rectangular, page-sized tray containing a jelly-like substance. There was a special aniline dye in the hectograph pencils used to make the master copies for our coloring pictures.

Our picture-making process involved putting a thin paper over an outline picture in the big book, then tracing it using a hectograph pencil. To transfer the image, the tracing would be placed face down on the gelatin surface, remain there briefly, then be removed. Next, we could press a clean sheet of paper over the gelatin, leaving it briefly before peeling it off. Presto, a new outline picture to color with crayons.

We loved to sing and found great enjoyment in learning, by rote, many of the old songs in the *Golden Songbook*. Most of our teachers could sing. The ones who could not carry a tune very well would ask a child to start the song or sing a verse alone. It worked!

Each spring there was a town spelling bee where town kids and those from rural schools would compete.

Before the end of our eighth grade year we had to go to Ewing High School to take County written exams in order to get tuition for public high school. I never heard of a failure because the tuition was needed by the high school. Our parents would receive a letter from the county saying we passed, and that our tuition would be paid to Ewing Public School beginning in September. These exams were easy for me but I recall not knowing what condiment meant. The question was on the physiology exam. Since then, I know pepper is a condiment.

Lunch boxes or buckets were a necessity at a rural school. Very few kids had one of the colorful store-bought metal boxes with handles and a few used a heavy, brown paper bag, but most of us used tin syrup pails renamed as lunch buckets. For one or two persons, a half-gallon size would be used. The gallon size was usually large enough for a family.

When it came lunch time, the teacher would have us put away our books to clear our desks, then say something like, "Rise and pass." We'd single-file to a shelf in the coatroom to pick up our lunch bucket, which had been placed there when we arrived at school, then return to our desks to eat. If the kids of one family shared a bucket, and when the weather was nice, the boys would grab their sandwich and run outside with it.

Our school lunch bucket was the gallon size tin syrup pail. Its wire handle made it easy to carry when walking or riding the horse. However, I recall on a few occasions that the handle separated from the bucket when the horse galloped. That meant getting off the horse to pick up the bucket. The bucket rolled in the dirt but a tight lid usually protected the contents. If the lid came off, the ground was sprinkled with sandwiches. If the handle was lost, well that was another problem. Picture it, trying to get back on the horse while trying to grasp a bucket with no handle, especially if one was riding bare-back! If there were two or more of us, it helped.

The contents of our school lunch bucket? Sandwiches filled with meat, jelly or peanut butter. On the not-so-good days, it would be syrup which made the bread soggy. Mom was great for oranges, but an orange in the can and a syrup sandwich did not mix too well. We tried to get the sticky, flattened bread down without being seen by the other kids. Wax paper was unknown in our house.

Vandalism was not unheard of in those days though the word itself was. One time neighborhood boys lifted a farm cultivator to the top of the small red horse barn on the school property. On finding a machine on the roof, the teacher knew it was a prank and asked the big boys to bring it down. The guilty pranksters, or someone, hauled it away at night so as not to be exposed.

Whether it was Halloween, I do not recall, but one morning the teacher and early-comers found the school room ransacked and disordered. Ink had been tossed on the wall and spilled elsewhere. Blackboards were messed up and strewn about. The teacher's hand bell was found much later in a small attic space that was covered with a movable board. The teacher went home discouraged and her big farmer brother came to take over the classes. Kids snickered at his style of teaching. He had a sharp eye on the possible guilty parties, and he warned the guilty ones to confess before the day was over. I do not recall the outcome, but it was generally known who did the damage and they were treated with a wicked eye.

One of the highlights of the year was the annual Christmas program consisting of dialogs, singing, etc. We'd bring bed sheets and string them across the back to make a narrow stage. Everyone wanted to pull the curtains at stage time. Sometimes a box social would follow the program, which meant brightly decorated lunch boxes would be auctioned. Younger girls would watch bug-eyed to see who got the older girls' boxes.

Another special day was Valentine's Day. We'd exchange homemade or store-bought valentines. The teacher would provide a brightly colored box decorated with crepe paper that had a slit in the top. We would draw names to see who could be Mail Man when it was time to distribute the contents. Heart cookies topped with red sugar never failed to appear at the Valentine party.

The end-of-the-year picnic was a fun day when nearly every family brought a potato salad, baked beans, pickles, buns, wieners, etc. The always-to-be-remembered-picnic-day was when Uncle John Bauer brought a five-gallon can of strawberry ice cream with plenty of cones to go with it. In those days, such a can was hard to pack. I can still see him removing the big tall can from a brown canvas bag. He had brought it from Ewing, about six miles away. Every kid swarmed around Uncle John and watched bug-eyed, squealing with delight. His daughter, Matilda, was our teacher, and she soon had us in order to await our turn for cones.

Yes, rural school days evoke many nostalgic memories. We had opportunities not found in the town schools. We learned from listening to other classes and we received individual attention.

It is regrettable that rural education is nearly a thing of the past. Few rural schools exist today.

BASEBALL GAMES

Every Sunday afternoon the neighbors would meet at a different farm for baseball games. I recall the old Fords going through the cottonwood grove to meet on the meadow east of the grove on those days. They were jolly good times for all.

MY DEAR FRIEND

rev. 2006

I can hardly think of my dear friend Frances Weibel, now Sr. Armella, without thinking of her Dad, Pa Weibel, the Patriarch of the family. Born in Alsace Lorraine, he was proud of the fact that everyone in the nearby community was aware of it. Sometimes we'd jokingly recall Pa Weibel's stories about Alsace Lorraine.

I can still see him sitting at his roll-top desk in the corner of the sitting room in their farm house. Everyone who came to their house would experience his, "Come here and let Francie show you what she can do." From the time she was small, he'd ask her questions, counting, naming presidents, whatever she might have learned along the way at her age level.

As time went on, Frances joined her sister in the small town public school. She was top student and excelled in math. I was a year younger and had trouble with math. Frances would help me.

I liked home economics but found algebra and geometry difficult. I recall her giving me her note books of algebra and geometry that followed the book we were using perfectly. In order not to copy, she'd explain the problems to me. During those two years, we became close friends. And, with her help, I passed those subjects.

Then I went to St. Mary's Boarding School, thirty miles away, for my junior and senior years.

I never intended to be a nun, but in my senior year I felt this call and discerned that it was real. I broke the news to Frances, who by this time had graduated and was staying home on the farm. Her words to me were spoken softly and sincerely. "It was what I always wanted to do, but I don't know how." Then we had long heart-felt talks about God and our ideals and life. I suggested she talk to Sister Dolores in O'Neill. She was willing.

Pa Weibel drove us to St. Mary's on a warm June day. He took the wheel of the old brown Model A and steered it with body erect, hands steady. One would have thought it was a Rolls Royce. Pa spent time down town while Frances talked with Sr. Dolores. She came home with an application.

Frances thought of coming with me to the convent, but her call was to the School Sisters of St. Francis in Milwaukee, Wisconsin, and her name was changed to Sr. Armella. At that time, Sisters in that order could come home every five years.

After various teaching assignments, Sister Armella taught mathematics for over forty years at Alveno College in Milwaukee, Wisconsin.

Frances, now Sr. Armella for over fifty years, and I have remained good friends throughout our lives. She, too, is now in retirement, still living in Milwaukee.

BEELART'S

Once or twice a year we'd visit Beelart's who lived north of town. Mom and Mrs. Beelart were friends and talked a mile a minute. Mrs. Beelart was Bohemian, or something like it, and spoke a very broken English. We often wondered how Mom could understand her. In the summer we would pick apples from their orchard and bring them home for eating or canning. One year they had blueberries, something very different for us.

LEYDEN'S

One time Mom and we kids were invited to Mrs. Leyden's for dinner. Mary drove us to their place up west. The women visited while we kids play outside. Finally, it was mealtime. The table was loaded and the final treat was cake **and** pie. I took a piece of each and devoured it in usual fashion.

Later when we were outside, Mary told me I should **not** have taken both cake and pie, only one. Words followed and I took her hand and bent her fingers back in the fight. She withdrew to the car and we kids played on.

A while later I saw Mary with a handkerchief tied around her fingers. My conscience pricked, thinking I had broken her fingers. I was too proud to ask or apologize. Boy, was it a relief when Mom came to go home and Mary drove the car as usual with no signs of bandage on her fingers! I think she was trying to scare me.

THE STILL

During Prohibition days in the 1920s, it was not uncommon for families to seek other ways to supplement their income. Bootlegging was a way some families made a living.

We had heard of stills, but only in faraway places. Then there were rumors that one or more could be close to our home, that booze, or hooch as it was sometimes called, was being peddled in small flasks at barn dances and parties.

One day I recall walking home from our rural school with my sister and brother. The topic of conversation, when we got home, was about a visit of Federal Agents to the still a mile away. They had dynamited the booze factory and arrested the man responsible for it.

Times were difficult for all of us, but none of us dreamed our neighbors were at it. Of course, we all felt especially sorry for his wife and small children and wondered what would happen to them! After all, we kids were those kids' classmates and friends!

On our way home from school the next day, Bill, Ann and I walked the road past their house. No one was home so we ventured over to the low, brown-roofed structure that we knew as the icehouse. As we neared it, we got a whiff of whiskey. We looked into the open doorway and saw several big fifty-gallon wooden barrels, kind of buried in straw and dirt, all blasted, with rye mash scattered all over. Never had I suspected the icehouse south of the home was anything but an icehouse—quite a sight for us kids! We trudged on home to relate our findings

Later, our Mother went to court on behalf of this man as his wife was pregnant with another child. The family was permanently grateful. They got through the depression like the rest of us, better for the ordeal.

MYSTERY MAN

When growing up on our farm in the Nebraska sandhills during the 1930s drought and depression era, there were opportunities to share the ups and downs with neighbors, relatives, and any stranger who might drop by.

One afternoon, on a summer day, a good-looking stranger came to the door. As with most anyone in those days, he was invited in. Teck took over. I recall her talking to him in the dining room, as we looked on from a distance.

What he posed as a business I don't recall, but because of the friendly conversation between Teck and the man, we kids thought he might be asking her for a date. Not so!

It seems he asked questions about our mailman's route. Now, this was a thorny question. Our mailbox was among those that would be cut off if the route changed.

A trip to Ewing that evening revealed through home town gossip, that the visitor was an FBI agent who was scouting for the writer of an anonymous letter. The recent mail route change had left some disgruntled patrons and the recipient of the nasty letter was out-to-get-'em. The incident apparently died peacefully as we didn't hear of anyone going to the pen. The visit of the FBI man gave the town something to chew on for a long time.

SPITTLER'S

Spittler's was located mid-way on Main Street in the town of Ewing. The tiny post office was next to their establishment and located on the corner. It was hard to say just what their establishment was. Anything in the way of a machine related object could be obtained there, whether it be a screw for a cream separator, a mowing machine, or a Ford car. Jack and Lee Spittler operated the Spittler Brothers Store which, at first sight, looked like a mammoth junk shop, with one exception. Lee or Jack knew where everything was and, given time, they could usually locate a needed machine or part.

Outside the shop was the gas pump and air tube for filling tires. Inside, located in the middle of disorganized machinery, cars and parts, was a small office. As a child accompanying my Mom or Aunt Tress, who'd stop to have a word with friendly Jack, we'd stand in the office and chat. I looked at the open roll-top desk laden with books, maps, bills, catalogs and diverse materials, wondering how anyone could possibly find anything. The walls of the small office were dusty and greasy. Pictures and old calendars, clippings and junk hung in disarray on their musty surface. Jack always had good humor, it seemed, and had time for a friendly word. Lee was less often seen.

Perhaps he was the one who got the work done. On Sundays, he sang in St. Peter's Church Choir. In my mind, this made Lee a special, highly respected parish member.

The farmers who patronized Spittler Brothers could usually depend on them to get the materials they needed.

Years after they passed on, I was told of several auctions and sales that were held at the site of their former store. Many an antique and heirloom must have passed though its doors.

§ § § § § § § § §

1960s
My dear friend
Sr. Armella Weibel

1976
Sr. Barty and Sr. Armella

3

God's Brat

Poetry Prayers & Tongue Twisters

A joy of retirement – time to reflect and to write
©2006 Steph's Studio

My attempts to write poetry are mostly reflections during quiet prayer times. They are enjoyable times.

Tongue twisters were efforts to calm noisy thoughts or to bring about sleep.

Poetry
Prayers
&
Tongue twisters

Titles in the order in which they are printed:

A PRAYER FOR EVERY DAY

adapted from *A Cathedral*

Oh, God:
Give me strength to live another day;
Let me not turn weak before its difficulties
  or betray its duties;
Let me not lose faith in humanity;
Keep me sweet and sound of heart,
  in spite of ingratitude or meanness;
Preserve me from minding little stings
  or giving them;
Help me to keep my heart clean
  and to live so honestly and fearlessly
  that no outward failure can dishearten me
  or take away the joy of conscious integrity;
Open wide the eyes of my soul
  that I may see good in all things;
Grant me this day some new vision of your truth;
Inspire me with the spirit of joy and gladness,
  and make me the cup of strength
  to all who suffer;
In the name of our Redeemer,
  Jesus Christ, our Lord. Amen

»»»«««

AT AGE SIXTY-EIGHT

1979 or 1980

I celebrate myself and sing with gratitude .....
for life's continuous blessing
of all the good things of this world.

The good things, what are they?
The miracle of each moment
as we pass along life's way ......

The healing of past .....
the grace of each moment today .....
and the hope that brings promise tomorrow.

The beauty of life in the now
I find in each person and creature.
Praise God who has shown me how.

»»»«««

BIG BEN

I consider this to be my very first long poem
written for a YMCA Elderhostel Class on writing
September, 1990 Estes Park, Colorado

Standing cold and self assured
  on my desk this dreary day,
Your dozen piercing eyes
  stare long and hard at me.
They join your rhythmic tick, tock
  to rouse in me temerity.
From a quiet meditation
  I'm stirred to prompt alert.
Your sudden clanging ears
  arouse in me uncertain fears.
A glance at rugged mountains westward
  brings calm tranquility
As I absorb an awesome presence
  Calling me to reflect eternity.

»»»«««

BIG HORN SHEEP

Reflections on a postcard picture
Marycrest - 1980s

Two big horn sheep
Sturdy, vigilant sentinels
Proudly posturing
on mountain peak.
Are you God's horned angels
Watching over us?

»»»«««

BIRTHDAY BLESSINGS

My version of a Birthday Beatitudes I have on a greeting card
Marycrest Chapel - 1980s

Happy are those who look forward to birthdays;
  they will have gladness of heart.
Peaceful are those who never fear aging;
  they are young at heart.
Graced be those who are thankful for all of life;
  their gratitude is on-going prayer.
Comforted are those who see roses not thorns;
  they shall know all good.
Valued be those who work for peace;
  Their efforts will circle the earth.
Favored are those who see beauty in all things;
  their small miracles will multiply.
Delighted are those who enjoy life
  with a sense of humor;
  they will laugh their way into heaven.
Praised be those who hope for a better tomorrow;
  they will make it so.
Joy to those who give and share;
  life will have meaning and peace.

»»»«««

BLESSED ARE THEY

Blessed are they
who look forward to birthdays,
they will have gladness of heart.
Blessed are they
who never fear aging,
they are hopeful and young in spirit.
Blessed are they
who are grateful for all life,
their gratitude is on-going prayer and praise.
Blessed are they
who trust God with all regrets,
he will take care of the past.
Blessed are they
who see roses, not thorns,
they shall know delight.
Blessed are they
who work for peace and justice,
their efforts will circle the earth.
Blessed are they
who see beauty around them,
their small miracles will multiply daily.
Blessed are they
who enjoy life with a sense of humor,
they will smile their way into heaven!

»»»«««

CHAPEL I

Queen of Peace Oratory at Marycrest
written October, 1991 - revised November, 1991

Thousands of bricks on chapel walls,
Revealing your age through gradual change
of color, texture, appearance—no two alike.

Each one growing, maturing, waiting, hoping,
As together you enhance the source of your strength,
Our Eucharistic God, enshrined in your midst.

Could it be that your special gifts encased in mortar
are maturing, mellowing, beautifying,
As you gaze kindly on one another
from opposite sides of your sacred dwelling?

Can we learn from you
to gaze lovingly at one another ...
To support one another, to heal one another ...
Yes, even draw forth life giving gifts
from the melting mortar of our hearts?

O God of bricks and mortar and people,
Live deeply in us as we strive to unify
in building up your Body—in glorifying your Name.
AMEN

»»»«««

CHAPEL II

Queen of Peace Oratory at Marycrest
1992

O Bricks, you speak to me of aging, agony and ardor.
Aging in different stages of life ...
All are displayed for us to ponder.

Your varied spots are the tell tale facts of growth:
    light, dark, small, middling,
        large, bulging, reposing, commanding,
            dominating, crouching, cringing,
    elongated, tall, short, stunted,
        fading, glowing, struggling, simmering,
            posing, emerging, maturing, dying ...
Each and all transforming inwardly and outwardly
  to form the mottling whole.

Such is life—black, white, brown, yellow, red ...
Each and all in touch with their Creator.

Can the strong uphold the weak?
Perhaps the Meek and Lowly will possess the land.
Is powerlessness the key?

»»»««««

CHIVALRY IS ALIVE

September 8, 2000

Chivalry, shining knights and perfect gentlemen,
Are they dead and gone forever?
Not so, not so! Amen, Amen.
Gray-haired nun says
"Never, never!"

"Prove it!" says the crowd.
"I found one," says the nun,
As she shouts it loud and clear.
He's truly a ray of God's sun!
His name is Manuel, a Jack-of-all-trades.
Many people know him well,
And of him they're not afraid.

The story goes like this:
Old nun drying clothes in laundry,
drops her panties on the floor.
Knight happens forth so jauntily!
Jump over, pass by, close his eyes?
No, a perfect gentleman.
He stooped, like knightly guys,
And picked up the old nuns panties.
With royal gesture, he presents the panties.
Embarrassed nun accepts, as if on a silver platter.

No, my friends,
Chivalry is not dead!
It lives on in humble Manuel !!!

»»»«««

ELDERHOSTEL

Reflection following Elderhostel at Golden, Colorado
July, 1992

Planning, anticipating, packing...
each and all a part of the fun of an Elderhostel.
Driving to Golden can be fun too ...
Until—rumble, rumble, rumble ...
the exhaust system sends a warning.
The Dodge can rest under the olive trees
until I've time to make telephone calls.

Classes are stimulating:
poetry, writing, storytelling, sharing...
cobwebs begin to fall from unused gray matter.
The cheer and chatter of friendly seniors
matches well the healthy humor of my friends.
And then—the sudden twist of a left ankle
while picking large juicy crab apples
stifles the fun-filled week.
Music and art will have to wait
as the Dodge and I slow down to recover.

And now as I repose and reflect
and move on a lifeless limb ...
Memories abound:
crab apples, jelly, kindly Seniors!

»»»««««

FATHER BRYAN

For our pastor's farewell party here at Marian Residence
June, 2004
Sung to the tune of Farmer in the Dell

Dear Bryan, you are leaving. We're sad to see you go,
But memories so good abound
From nineteen years review.

We loved you from the start. You took us all to heart!
The parish you did soundly build
As ever you took part

We thought you might be bishop,
But Rome thought otherwise.
You stayed with your beloved flock,
And lived the Jesus' life

For fun, your pal, the pick-up, Would take you out to fish.
No fancy trips or lavish treats
But fishing filled your wish.

With us you did play cards, And joined in all our fun.
Our simple meals you did enjoy.
We'll miss you, everyone.

You gave to us your time
In ministering to us,
In giving us the sacraments
And extra masses, too.

Ogallala will be blest, As you give them of your best.
God bless you with His love and care
With you we remain in prayer.

»»»««««

GLISTENING WEB

Written when I was Minister to the Elderly
at Marycrest Convent in Denver, Colorado
written and Published in the Fall, 1991
"Aging and the Human Spirit Newsletter"
VT-Med. Branch, Galveston, Texas

O God, Glistening Web,
stronger than welded weavings
You are our many ladders,
enabling us
to climb, stretch, search ...
til we are caught
securely in your love.

»»»«««

GOD PROVIDES

Queen of Peace Oratory
April, 1993

The morning paper says it's April Fool's Day.
And what does that mean?
For me it's the foolishness of
Wasting time ....
In listening to chirping, singing birds ....
In quiet moments of gazing early daffodils ....
In picking tender dandelion greens
for spring cleansing of winter clogs ....
In feeling the fresh green grass
spring from gentle rain ...
In letting the blue sky lift my thoughts and prayer
to One alone
Who provides the foolishness of April 1.

»»»«««

GREEN

Elderhostel Writing Class at Golden, Colorado
July, 1992

Green gives me hope ...
Loudly and clearly it says tomorrow will be better.
I see it in each slender blade of grass,
in green, growing meadows.

Green gives me hope ...
Tall trees wave their thousands of signs of hope.
As each leaf speaks.
It adds to the total gift we receive this day.

Green gives me hope ...
Even the butterfly sprinkles this gift of life
as it dances among tall green weeds
of a hope-laden vacant yard.

Green gives me hope ...
A teen-age boy attired in green shorts
gives life and joyful hope
as he jogs along the open road.
All creation proclaims God's gifts of hope.

Green gives me hope ...
A pause at the green light gives time for reflection.
Silently it says
Fear not the red, God is alive and well !
Yes, green gives me hope!

»»»«««

HOPE I

Queen of Peace Oratory
1990s

Tall, green plant
Your many-fingered leaves reach outward and upward
In open embrace of the wide open world ...
A world in need of healing and a kindly touch.

God is your sturdy trunk,
nourishing those wide open arms,
strengthening them with gentleness.

Tall, green plant,
do keep on feeding our hungry, needy world
with faith and hope and love
to make it whole again.

»»»«««

HOPE II

House of Prayer
March, 1992

Gray, barren trees
  tall, straight, unyielding in your winter garb
Sun's bright rays
  barely change your drabness
Winter birds do little
  to move your unbending arms.

Then, lo, bleak March changes!

The sun grows warmer
Strong March winds alone
  wield power to shake one's stiffened bones
Soft breezes blow, branches gently sway
Spring is on its way.

Buds burst open in silence
In brief moments
  barren branches bear blooms
Soft winds shake maturing buds to the ground
Footsteps crunch these signs of spring
Hungry earth receives such trampled nourishment
Spring is on its way
Hope is renewed.

»»»«««

HORSEBACK MEMORIES

A Spiritual Journey exercise at Elderhostel art class
1991

Five years old.
I get to ride pasture—with my Dad.
He hoists me behind weathered brown leather saddle
Under which a colorful Indian blanket
hugs the handsome sorrel's back.
Dad leads Dan to the pasture gate
north of our white frame house.
Unlatching the wire gate, we proceed and then wait
while Dad closes the barb wire latch.
Mounting his favorite horse,
I circle my arms around Dad's blue overalled waist,
And we're off to the big pasture to check the cattle.

The sorrel's step is gentle and I feel secure,
until Dad says, "Hold on tight"
and, "Giddyap."
Dan glides forward in a graceful lope.
As the saddle back bounces up and down
on my straddled, bare legs,
I hear pinch, pinch.
My tender skin feels pinch, pinch.
I want to scream, "It pinches! Stop! Go slow!"
but my thoughts say, "Dad's time is precious,
he's got to check the cattle;
he can't walk the horse just for me."

Then Dad's voice pipes out,
"Are you still there?"
His words are kind encouragement to hang on,
And I answer, "Yes, Dad, I'm here"
even though I hesitate to say, "...but it hurts."

The alternating of the horse's
gentle gallop and walk continues
as Dad counts cattle and checks their needs.

Back home an hour or so later,
Dad lifts me from the horse
as I say something like, "It was fun."

Inside our house
I show my blistered, bloody legs to my mother.
She says, "Child, why didn't you tell Dad
to walk the horse?"

Today, sixty-eight years later,
I draw a picture of Dad and me on the sorrel.
Memories flow.
"Are you still there?"
"Why didn't you say Stop?"
Pondering this picture long and ardently,
a long overdue insight strikes sharply!

Why didn't you utter Slow Down
when, over the years,
people hurt you knowingly or unknowingly.
Owning my vulnerability,
I recognize my fear and hesitation to say,
"Stop! It hurts!"

At seventy-three, I'm learning to say,
"Slow down, be gentle with me."
Yes, I'm also learning to be
more patient and gentle with others,
a life-long process.

»»»«««

"I"

Professor Maxwell's Creative Writing Class
February, 1994
His comments: "Meek and tentative. Express your feelings.
Don't count on beeps to do it." Maxwell

I belong to God
His loving care surrounds me
even when I fail.

Broken, burnt, darkened
God's touch heals slowly.

Go forth now and heal
one another.

~~~~~

I am a hay seed
nurtured in Nebraska sand hills.
Hayseeds bring new life.

The seed must die
before it can become
full-grown green hay.

»»»«««
~~~~~

INSPIRATION

Marycrest Cabin in Cold Creek Canyon, Colorado
June, 1992

Strong, sturdy pine, swaying tall in brisk wind,
are you exercising for warmth?
Un-threatened by restless, gloomy clouds above,
your strong healthy branches
flow gracefully from sturdy, enduring trunk.
Your companions of motley sizes and shades of green
sway in unison with you.
Could you be their mentor, inspiration, confidant ...
As you are to me this day?
PLUNK!! Your pine cone lands at my feet ...
a prompt and sacred reply!

»»»««««

LAUGHTER

2006

L—lifts and liberates
A—activates adrenaline
U—ups our unconscious
G—gives graciously
H—harmonizes heartily
T—thinks thankfully
E—enables and enlarges
R—radiates and ripples

»»»««««

LOCUST TREE

Elderhostel at St. Scholastica, Canon City, Colorado
June, 1993

Lovely, lacy-leafed locust tree
your long slender arms
hold many fingered branches
reaching outward, upward
in a spiraling stretch toward the sun.

Sideward branches
form a green holey umbrella
to sift sun rays
that gentle us
who repose below.

Looking upward
a restful blue sky
filters through the fragile leaves
calming us with peace, joy, love
endless gifts to make us whole.

»»»«««

LORD, YOU ARE MY ROCK

Lord, you are my ROCK!
A rock is strong and impenetrable.
It remains anchoring and faithful, always there
for what ever needs it may serve,
to be sat on for rest
or merely to be looked at for inspiration.
My particular rock
allows the ants and beatles to play games on its surface,
and they find warmth and comfort in its crevices.
A rock is stable and enduring,
weathering the winds and rains
in an indomitable fashion.
Lightning and thunder are never a threat to a rock.
When my inner fears
and insecurities
reach a peak,
my Rock can be a calming force,
bringing peace and tranquility,
as its shares Its endless inner strength with me.
A rock lets green, lush moss
grow on its surface.
This reminds me that lush, green life
can be mine
by clinging to my faithful, life-giving ROCK.

»»»«««

MATTIE

House sitting and dog sitting
Mattie was a German Shepherd dog
at the Bass residence in Denver, Colorado
July, 1992

I am loved!
Contentment is my life.
Joy, excitement, well being
Are fringe benefits.
My home is one of peace.
I am loved!
Devotion to my family
Is a source of pride in me.
I am loved!

Playtime for Mattie

»»»«««

MY PRAYER

Friday, April 26, 1996

Thank you, God —
  for a good night's sleep.
To feel rested
  is to know your blessing.

A new day's call
  to wake up and live now
  has a new ring of joy and hope.
I go forth
  fortified by nourishment
  in your Sacrament of Love
  to meet the challenges
  of a fallible Friday.

Such cherished challenges
  they prove to be,
To offer a smile, a touch,
  each with heart felt care,
To each frail, saintly senior
  who receives
  this smallest sign of love
  with a smiling face
  and grateful heart.

To serve saintly seniors
  is to receive
  their goodness and wisdom
  a hundred fold.
AMEN

»»»«««

MYSTERY

Reflection that brightened a pity party one day
Marian Chapel, Alliance, Nebraska
2006

Why am I bereft of special gifts,
of speech and sparkle?
Their absence in my life
commands attention,
As I long for esteemed respect.
If desires could earn
such valued aid to Christlike action,
Then need for peace and justice
in our world
Would long ago have ceased!

Alas, God's gifts are freely given.
I must be content with mystery
as I grasp the question
And do the little things
that are God's love and mercy
put in my way.
I am happy with these gifts.

»»»«««

OUR FATHER

Retreat at Marycrest, Denver, Colorado
August, 1992

With hands out-stretched, palms upward,
fingers apart, I pray:

Our Father, we praise you and honor you
for what you are—a Father and Mother to us.
Through these pleading, praising hands,
let your grace pour forth through these fingers
to a needy, desperate world.
See the spaces as symbols
of our emptiness and openness to receive.

Father, let fall the faith, hope and love
that will bring about your Kingdom.
May your name be honored.
Let justice and peace reign in the world.

Let rain fall
on drouth stricken, thirsty continents.
Let forgiveness and reconciliation
erase friction and violence.
Let families and children
find love and security.
Let the sick, elderly, and grieving
find strength and solace.
Let those who are discouraged and despairing
find hope.

Look into the hearts of the good
  and let them want to be better.
Look into the hearts of the tempted
  and give them strength.
Look into the hearts of the evil ones
  and offer them the desire and will to repent.

Let people everywhere
  touch one another
  with your healing power.
Those who are fearful, hurting, unfree
Father, let all humanity
  find life and freedom in Jesus,
  Your gift to us.

AMEN

»»»«««

PSALM 1

I wrote this Psalm during the Heritage Retreat in Denver in July, 2001.The retreat was given by Sisters Chretienne Nibbelke and Willibrord Yeuken from Divine Providence Province in the Netherlands.During this retreat we reflected on the life and times of our foundress, Magdalen Damen, and how we continue to live out our heritage in the first year of the twenty-first millennium. It was printed in a small booklet which contained all the poems, prayers, and psalms of those who attended this retreat.

My soul,
My whole being
Give glory to you, my God,
You who have loved me into being.

With contrite heart
I come to you, my Love,
For failures in my daily life.
How can I forget?

You have forgiven all.
You desire not my guilt
But the gift of my tears
And open loving heart.

While maturing, oh, so slowly,
You watched my every step
And saved me from
The world's false values.

Then, my God, my all,
You invited me to be your bride.
Could this be real? A true call?
Questioned my inner being.

A Franciscan bride of yours
Helped me discern that yes,
You were really calling me!
Humbly grateful, I gave you my **Yes**.

From age sixteen to eighty-two,
You have been a faithful
Father, friend and lover.
How can I repay you?

In my graying years,
You keep me green and growing
As I try to do your bidding.
All glory be to you my God!

Not one thought, word, deed
Was done without your help,
Yet self-love sometimes said,
"Twas mine, I did it."

Oh God, you continue
To love me into life;
The quiet times with you
Are filled with gentle love.

Oh God, I am unworthy
Of your faithfulness
As I go about my daily rounds.
Shine through me to those in need.

»»»«««

QUIET DAY, QUIET PRAYER

Retreat at St. Walburgas in mountains NW of Denver
Spring, 1992

Quiet day, quiet prayer,
O blessed solitude.
Past hurts, dreams, visions,
coming to full circle
Strengthening the boundaries of my life.
Jesus' own arms enfolding,
calling me to a self-assurance
that directs me outward
to others in forgiveness,
to others in pain,
to those close to me,
to those outside,
who long for and wait for
someone to care, to bless, to listen.
O Lord, fill my cup
that I may share its love
and bring about Your kingdom.

»»»«««

RED TULIPS

Queen of Peace Oratory, Marycrest in Denver
1980s

Tall red tulips, interspersed with fragrant lilacs
giving worship to our Eucharistic Lord,
Teach us how to stand tall
in faithful service to our Creator
Let your inner beauty touch our lives
as it reaches to God within us.

»»»«««

SAGGING FENCE & GRAZING SHEEP

Rocky Mountains
Summer, 1991

Sagging wire fence - tottering fence posts
Faithful guardians
of peaceful pasture.

~~~~~~~

Grazing sheep
munching rich, green grass,
Your scattered presence,
like white robed monks in prayer,
reflect
contentment, freedom, peace...

»»»«««
~~~~~~~

SENIOR CENTER

early 1990s

This is the day I choose for writing.
Off to the Center with book and bag.
After greeting and sharing,
I choose the activity room.
At one end of the long table
are two chess players,
quietly pondering their moves.
I sit down at the opposite end of the long tables,
remove note book and papers from bag,
and begin to read *Prime Time.*
No stopping 'til it's finished!
I came to write!
Next I pick up nursing home schedules
and revise them.
I came to write!
A senior friend comes by to chat.
I came to write!
By this time I'm hungry and eat.
I came to write!
Woe is me!
Distraction and procrastination
will never get me started
until I vow:
I WILL write!

»»»«««

SHAKE -AWAKE

early 1990s

Shake-wake—that's it—A small clock
that vibrates at the time you set.
Colorful ads had me believing
I'd be lifted off the pillow. Not so!
There's a kind of vibrative buzz
that must touch my inner sleeping equipment
in some way, and then I am awake,
without being shaken to pieces.

It's an interesting, mysterious piece of machinery
that must have had a clever inventor,
One who may have been deaf,
and or who understood what it means
to be a late comer.

It is with a sense of gratitude that I respect
my little black clock and give it credit
for getting me to morning prayer on time.
Gone are the excuses—I overslept,
Didn't hear the alarm—and others.

Shake-Awake provides the discipline I need
to begin the day by getting up on time.
I look forward to many more happy days
with the help of my little getter-upper.

This twenty-four-dollar helper
has one cause for a bit of anxiety
The day it has to be sent to Hong Kong for repair.
It is not guaranteed forever!!

»»»«««

THE FOUNTAIN

Elderhostel Retreat
St. Scholastica Retreat Center, Canon City, Colorado
June, 1993

Pure, sparkling water, gift of the moment
You speak to me of tears,
  growth, nourishment, life ...
Tears of struggles in many births,
  infancy, childhood, growing years,
  adulthood, age of wisdom ...
Again and again ...
  flowing out to cleanse, purify,
  beautify, rejoice ...
Can one ever overcome,
  be courageous, even blossom?
The sparkling fountain of rhythmic,
  tinkling, dancing streams sings:
"Yes ... yes ...
  you were so from the womb !!!
  Realize it, acknowledge it;
  respect, love your every effort.
  Each one is a diamond shining brightly
  as my own drops of recycling nourishment."
My better self speaks:
  "True, take pride in God's transforming efforts,
    enjoy the fruits of your growing up,
      share them as you receive from others."
Lord, help me to do so. AMEN

»»»«««

TONGUE TWISTERS

Marycrest, Denver, Colorado
1980s

Tenacious tenants taught Tauism to teenagers.
They tattooed tattered tottelers ...
Telling tall tales ... trying to test tensions tactfully.
Tall Timothy titillated timelessly
 'til Tao teacher took time to teach tacitly
 thus training Timothy to think thankfully.
This tantalizing treatment took time
 to thoroughly thwart Timothy's titillating tremors.
Total thankfulness
 terminated Tau teacher's touching treatment.

☺ ☺ ☺ ☺ ☺

Petty, paltry, putrid power pulling
 poor people to poverty.
Petty, paltry, putrid power pushing, pulling
 precious powerless persons.
Petty, paltry, putrid power pushing, pointing
 past the placid poor.
Petty, paltry, pandering, powerful, partial
 to the polished politic.
Petty, paltry, pandering, powerful
 partying pitifully.
Petty, paltry, pandering, powerful,
 please ponder in prayer.

»»»«««

TONGUE TWISTING TONGUE TWISTERS

- ☻ Abandoned apples
  appearing approachable arouse appetites aggressively.
- ☻ Dear doggies
  digest double drumsticks dutifully.
- ☻ German grandma
  gives greedy gophers generous gristles in grits.
- ☻ Jolly Jennie jabbers jokingly
  as Jets join jaggling joggers jeopardizing jazzy jesters.
- ☻ Slithering snake
  slobbers slovenly, swishing and swerving silently.
- ☻ Yodeling yaks yap, yabber, yawl and yawn yearly.
- ☻ Zapping zanders zap zesty zinging zombies.

»»»«««

TRINITY

Marycrest Cabin in Cold Creek Canyon, Colorado
August, 1994

Tiny humming birds, you come in threes
identical except one red throat.
Flitting, flying, darting,
you lightly, swiftly glide among the pines
from one sweet, red feeder to the other.
You are friendly, happy, care free.
One of you even draws nectar
from the feeder nestled in my hand.
O, how I love to hold you in my hand.
Which one of the Trinity are you, O tiny one?
The answer comes: All Three in one.

»»»«««

TWO SMALL POEMS

I've yet to write a long poem
February 12, 1984

I belong to God
His loving care surrounds me
even when I fail.

Broken, burnt, darkened
God's touch heals slowly ...
Go forth now and heal one another.

»»»«««

TWO VALIANT MEN

For about six weeks we watched two young men clean and paint the inside and outside of the water tower across the street from our Marian Residence dining room window. The day they made their last trip down, several of us went out to cheer them. Theresa, our administrator, presented them a colorful certificate upon which was printed this jingle written just for them.

August, 2005

Two valiant men on a flying trapeze
Worked day after day in a high stifling breeze
Swinging and swaying with greatest of ease
As they painted and painted in total peace.

The tower is high, oh so high,
But they tackled the job with a zest
And nary a person heard ever a sigh
As they courageously gave of their best.

Oh, yes, the aged nuns in Convent nearby
Kept vigil by watching and sending up prayer.
The white glistening tower, now a majestic sight
As the town's proud landmark, oh so bright.

»»»«««

WELCOME

written for brother Bill's family gathering in the 1990s
Sing to the tune of Farmer in the Dell

We welcome all of us - We welcome all of us
Hi ho ding derry do - We welcome all of us!

'Tis good to see you all - 'Tis good to see you all
Hi ho ding derry do - We're going to have a ball!

Our memories they are good - Our memories they are good
Hi ho they are so good - We lived as best we could!

We have our up-and-downs - We have our up-and-downs
Hi ho ding derry do - We laugh instead of frown!

Our Dad must smile at us - Our Dad must smile at us
Hi ho ding derry do - He'd not want us to fuss!

Dad never made a fuss - Dad never made a fuss
Hi ho ding derry do - Once in a while he'd cuss!

And so we learn to live - And so we learn to live
Hi ho ding derry do - We laugh and love and live!

And when we go our way - And when we go our way
Hi ho ding derry do - God's with us every day!

We place our trust in him - We place our trust in him
Hi ho ding derry do - Our faith will never dim!

We'll always be in touch - We'll always be in touch
Hi ho ding derry do - We love each other much!

Before we say goodbye - Before we say goodbye
Hi ho ding derry do - We'll be happy til we die!

»»»«««

4

God's Brat

Haiku Poetry

Sr. Kathryn's Version

1993

Haiku is one of the most important forms of traditional Japanese poetry. Haiku is, today, a 17-syllable verse form consisting of three metrical units of 5, 7, and 5 syllables. In Japanese, this convention is a must, but in English, which has variation in the length of syllables, this can sometimes be difficult. In languages other than Japanese, there is NO consensus in how to write Haiku-poems.

Haiku-poems can describe almost anything, but you seldom find themes which are too complicated for normal PEOPLE'S recognition and understanding. Some of the most thrilling Haiku poems describe daily situations in a way that gives the reader a brand new experience of a well-known situation."

—above information obtained from HAIKU for PEOPLE at http://www.toyomasu.com/haiku/

RETREAT

Breckenridge, Colorado
Leuthy's Cabin
May, 1987

•Tall pine tree
dying with dignity
as outstretched arms
cry Abba Father.

•Two swallows
playing sky games
reveal to me
how God pursues with love.

•Neighbors lights
shining through the lattice
like eyes of the Beloved
searching for me.

•Nuns gleaning fire wood
Hark! An Angelus bell?
No! 'Tis a picture memory.

•Kindling wood
"Angelus bell"
What joy!
You are redeemed!

•Otto Luethy
your dying here
has made more sacred
this hallowed, peaceful place.

•Swift running stream
delight to eye and ear
God's cleansing life
erasing darkness
restoring light.

•Full moon
shining through
tall, swaying pines,
God's presence
obscured at times
by cloudy self
and withering world.

•Playing scrabble
reveals to me
God's loving
relentless pursuit.

CABIN

July, 1988

•Holy, happy hummingbird
hov'ring in mid-air
giving God all glory.

LUNCH HOUR

Sloan's Lake in Colorado
March, 1990

•Warm March day
gives me pause
noon walkers
slow their pace
around the lake.

•At noon break
carrot sticks
go crunch, crunch
between other healthy,
nutritious snacks.

•Lone fisher couple
your quiet repose
with lines in hand
speaks contentment.

•Long legged, skinny jogger
your wiry body
lapping 'round the lake.

•Blue-collar workers in
shiny pickup
eating hearty lunch
for afternoon strength.

•Overweight man
you strain to jog
as your belly shakes
Why not diet?

•Young mother, father
small boy, girl,
scampering dog,
happy family.

•Seventy-year-old nun
observing people
it's time
to get moving.

TECK'S POOL

Mesa, Arizona
January, 1991

•Aqua pool
rippling rhythmically
gently welcoming
eager swimmers.

•Chirping birds, warm sun
blue sky, quiet day
all reflect God's love.

MARYCREST CHAPEL

Denver, Colorado
1990s
Sen is a young OSF Sister from Vietnam

•Sen's bright altar cloth
a world of blood and fire
calling all to repent.

•Red glowing wall hanging
projecting violence and pain
contaminating all.

•Bright reddish banner
blazing blood and violence
repent, world, repent.

•Sen's art is blood and pain
an urgent call to repent
Can we "yes" the call?

•Sens real gift of art
a display of bloody anger
a call to repent or die.

MARYCREST

Queen of Peace
House of Prayer
April, 1992

•Grassy knoll
green tree
invitation to reflect.

•Warm May's days gift
spirea, peony, iris
nature's fashion show

•Green, growing trees
in many hues of hope
spring awakens life.

•Humming fan
cooling breeze
quiet day
an airplane hum
breaking monotony.

•Silent chapel
whirring fan
chirping birds
quiet Sunday.

•Whirring, whirling fan
standing upright
breathing cool air
into warm room.

•Jesus
Your image of death
on silent wall speaks:
You can do it too!

•Lovely Paschal candle
tall and purposeful
HOPE is your message.

•Retreat day:
reflect, repent, renew
prepare for tomorrow.

•Pink lilies
on tall leafed stems
in golden pot
elegance in bloom.

•Oh, twelve-eyed clock
staring into space
ticking off the time
How do I use it?

HOUSE SITTING

for Marie Mattivi
Denver, Colorado
May, 1992

Marie was an Austrian lady who married an Italian. She had one son.

•Fluttering, frolicking butterflies
on resurrection flight
raise us up!

•Community:
butterflies and blossoms
entertaining one another.

•Hospitality:
blooming lilac tree
embracing northbound
butterflies.

•Lilac party:
hostess in purple dress
entertaining Monarchs
in gold and black attire.

•O lilac tree, you welcome
playful Monarchs
to enhance your beauty.

•Spring movie:
bright lavender lilac bush
welcoming golden Monarchs

•Spring joy:
purple lilac tree
hosting nectar party
for thirsty Monarchs.

•God's glory and goodness
shines in purple tree
alive with Monarch butterflies.

•God, you reveal yourself
in spring lilacs
as You welcome Monarchs
from the South.

•The lilac tree
God's garden
where dancing butterflies
show us how to play.

•Lilac tree abloom
God's playground
for dancing golden butterflies.

•Welcome North, O Monarchs
your long journey
from the South
energizes you (and us).

•Golden, happy butterflies
play tag
among purple lilac blooms.

•Crystal wind chimes
casting sunny reflections
in silent prayer room.

•Dancing sunspots
in silent room
Mysterious source?
playful porch wind chimes.

•Six o'clock A.M.
delicious silence
solitude
God, speak to me!

•Tinkling crystal wind chimes
harmonize
with gentle darting sun bursts
on the wall.

•Six-thirty A.M.
God speaks in silence
even if I doze
wake up and live.

•God, you share your beauty
in happy butterflies
and blossoms.

HOUSE OF PRAYER

various times
1990s

•Droning motor
of overhead plane
breaking the silence
of a quiet day.

•Gathering clouds
on warm day
will you sprinkle
the earth
and brighten our way?

•Queen of Peace
haven of hope
help for the seeker
powerhouse of prayer.

•Tabernacle
God's Eucharistic home
burning candle
live red rose.

•Tabernacle
home of peace, passion, prayer
hope for the seeker
help for the weary.
God is present.

5

God's Brat

Church Bulletin Columns

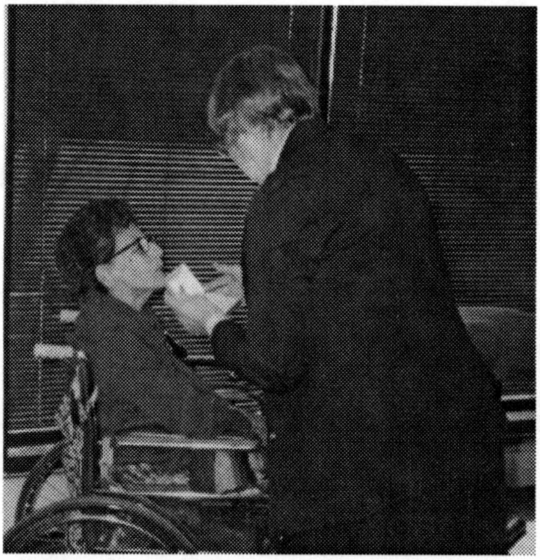
1980s – Minister to the Elderly

In my retired years, 1978–2004, I worked for St. Mary Magdalene Parish, Denver, Colorado, as Minister to the Elderly in nursing homes. For a short period of time, in 1988 and 1989, I wrote Church Bulletin Columns for that parish. On the following pages are some of those Columns.

Church Bulletin Columns

Titles in the order in which they are printed

A Story
A Wise Person Never Blows One's "Knows"
Advent
Advent, a Time of Hope
Advent, the Third Sunday of
All Saints-All Souls
Caught in the Act of Caring
Easter Tide
Evangelization
Hope is Alive
Lent
Love Your Neighbor as Yourself
Peacemaking Day by Day
Perseverance
Sign of Hope
The Present Moment
Wellness and Aging

A STORY

A Story is printed below to offer you an insight of how I felt about my work during those "retired years." I felt I was given the mission of serving my parish through serving its elderly members. Through my Columns, I served the whole parish as well.

> A disciple came to the Holy One and said, "There is something I do not understand. It took God six long, endless days to create the world. Look at it! It's terrible. It's corrupt. It's cruel. It's inhuman."
>
> The Holy One looked at the disciple for a long time and then asked, "Can you do better?"
>
> At that point the disciple fell silent. She knew what she wanted to say, and finally she summoned the courage to say it. " I think … YES!, Yes, I could build a better world."
>
> "Yes?" the Holy One shouted. "Then what are you waiting for? Get busy! Go to work! Begin! Begin immediately!"
>
> –*Author Unknown*

THINK PEACE—LIVE PEACE!

♡ ✞ ♡ ✞ ♡

A WISE PERSON NEVER BLOWS ONE'S "KNOWS"

October 2, 1988—27th Sunday in Ordinary Time

The above title was the answer to a Jumble Puzzle I worked on while riding Amtrak and enjoying the scenery.

This answer amused me briefly, but within moments I was reflecting seriously on the clever caption. Childhood recollections of bragging cropped up. Remember when you were the best speller—the best reader—the best runner—you could ride a horse bare back—and a dozen other such proud memories? These healthy, sometimes overly proud "knows" were not too difficult to recall.

But reviewing such bragging as one struggled through adolescence, adulthood, middle age, and now in old age was not so easy, nor did the recollections appear to be humorous. How often over the years my efforts to be better, stronger, smarter, faster, equal to, correct, just, right—you name it—I made the effort! Or so my revolving memories indicated.

Following quickly on these thoughts were those of, "Why such efforts to appear wise and in the know?" Was I proud, insecure, rebellious, jealous, dishonest, weak, fearful, cowardly? Whatever the reason, these ugly words were tapping on my memory as an inner voice was saying, "I love you the way your are—but there's a way to go—get busy—I'm not finished with you yet."

Honest pride versus false, excessive pride prompted recurring thoughts as I marveled at God's creation along the way. A concluding recollection to this meditation was that of a good friend, Sr. Borromea, who is wise in the Lord. When complimented one day for her meaningful reading of Scripture at Mass, she commented, "I **like** what I read."

Surely her simple, honest wisdom stems from St. Paul's word, "I know Him in whom I believe."

Lord, there is hope for each of us as you give our open hearts the grace to know you better, to love you more and to follow you more closely all the days of our lives. Thank you, Lord, for your patience.

♡ ♡ ♡

ADVENT

1988 or 1989

This week we journey with Mary as she ponders her Jewish heritage and the great things God has done in her. Hope rises in her heart as she quietly prays snatches of the Magnificat. Among them: "God's mercy is from generation to generation."

Hardly a day passes that some part of the world does not experience great tragedy, disaster, violence, suffering. A picture of Mr. Gorbachev addressing a large group of people showed extreme anguish on their faces. In the midst of such great suffering, these people are already experiencing hope, mercy and compassion of people throughout the world as open hearts reach out to help.

♡ ♡ ♡

ADVENT, A TIME OF HOPE

November 26, 1989—Christ the King

Advent is a time of hope. As life becomes more complex in the world we need the gift of hope more than ever.

An article on the *Five Hopeful Mysteries of the Rosary* hit my eye when reading a magazine on prayer. The authors, Sister Patricia Brockman, OSU, and Robert Gervasi, point out that in the overall fifteen mysteries of the rosary, there is a gap of Hope. In the spirit of the renewal of Vatican II, the authors give us the *Five Hopeful Mysteries* which dwell on the public life of Christ and complete the spirituality of the rosary:

The First Hopeful Mystery

Jesus is baptized and goes into the desert.

We reflect on the temptations and desert experience of Jesus, as we ponder our own struggles and call to hope in being purified and strengthened.

The Second Hopeful Mystery

Jesus invited His disciples to work for the Kingdom

This involves Community, a working together as we, like the early disciples, "seek the Kingdom first" in a hopeful way.

The Third Hopeful Mystery

Jesus shares with the crowds the good news of His Father's love

As Jesus was led to proclaim the good news of the Father's love, so we are invited to grow in and share that love. The world needs hope filled witnesses.

The Fourth Hopeful Mystery

Jesus heals the sick and raises the dead

Just as Jesus healed and forgave sins, so we must act and work with hope for justice, healing and life in a world where there is only oppression and death.

The Fifth Hopeful Mystery

Jesus invites His loved ones to share the final Passover

Jesus experiences the heaviness of parting, a sign of hope that Jesus understands our own suffering and humbly helps us just as He washed the disciples feet.

The authors say the greatest tribute we can pay to Mary is to include within the rosary her Son's message of hope, their reason for giving us the *Five Hopeful Mysteries.*

♡ ♡ ♡

ADVENT, THE THIRD SUNDAY OF

December 17, 1989—3rd Sunday of Advent

The beautiful Season of Advent is well on its way. The Third Sunday reminds us to "Rejoice in the Lord always: again I say, Rejoice!" The Lord is near as the entrance hymn proclaims. If we are living out the meaningful readings for Advent we have reason to rejoice. Our lives should be in the process of conversion and renewal as we prepare for the coming of our Savior.

The call to rejoice accompanies the call to hope. And we do see signs of hope in our world—leaders agreeing on peace efforts, walls coming down, people working for justice in various countries.

A few weeks ago I had occasion to spend a Sunday with an eighty-year-old Sister friend who had heard from her family in East Germany. Sharing her stories and her great joy over events in her country was a special gift that touched me deeply. Shortly after that I had occasion to visit with a friend of Polish descent. She asked me what I thought of news from Poland—the new Pope. Before I could respond, tears flowed down her cheeks and we both wept, a silent but deep sharing of joy and hope.

Such experience has pointed out the importance of not only sharing another's grief and suffering that touches and strengthens, but also of sharing and listening to others' joys, successes, hopes, that likewise encourage and enrich a person.

As Christians we are called to encourage one another not just by words but by our convictions. We can be a light in the darkness. We can radiate love. We can be a blessing to others by our very presence.

Lord, help as we try to proclaim your Kingdom to the world by our example. Come Lord Jesus!

♡ ♡ ♡

ALL SAINTS - ALL SOULS

November 13, 1988—33rd Sunday in Ordinary Time

November is the month we honor All Saints and All Souls. In our convent dining room on November first, there was a table display of statues and pictures honoring the Saints. Among the Mary's, Francis', Joseph's, there were photos of beloved parents, a brother, a sister, a nephew. There was a picture of twenty-nine-year-old Holly, niece of Sister Helen, who died of cancer after years of suffering. Now she wears the crown. Holly, pray for us!

Do we continue to think of our departed ones and pray to them as well as for them? Surely they are as close to the Lord as the vast number of book Saints. If their lives could be portrayed in a book or movie they would no doubt be as inspiring, or more so, because they were close to us in life. They fought the good fight and won.

Last month we lost two Sisters in one day, in the same convent in Nebraska. Our loss was their resurrection.

Sister Xavier had taught school for many years and, in retirement, was busy full time, helping where needed. As a faithful Religious and teacher, she will long be remembered for her cheerful patience and prayerfulness. Sister Xavier, pray for us!

Sister Theresa Hugpen came from Germany as a young Sister. She worked hard as a cook in our institutions nearly all her life. In retirement, she often visited the sick, elderly and imprisoned, and devoted herself to care of the chapel. Many letters now tell of the help Sister was to them. Sister Theresa, pray for us!

Surely in all families we can recall many such good lives. A passage from Karl Rahner, theologian, tells us how to remember our departed.

> "God is a God of the living, as Jesus tells us, and the separated are everlastingly current, and so can be and really are near to us in their silent love."

Dear Ones, pray for us, that we, too, can fight the good fight and earn the Crown!

♡ ♡ ♡

CAUGHT IN THE ACT OF CARING

September 24, 1989—25th Sunday in Ordinary Time

This title was found in a hospital bulletin. It was the caption for a small article by a passerby who witnessed the kind act of an employee to an elderly person in a parking lot.

The title recalled to me a recent experience in our Church parking lot after the nine o'clock mass. After friendly greetings and cheerful chatter, I walked toward the car and observed a mother with a babe in her arms being motioned to the car of a caring couple. The elderly man had lifted a colorful fuzzy animal from the car trunk and was gently offering it to the small child when I caught this act—a lovely one indeed! The child smiled with delight as small arms hugged the stuffed toy. Of course the kindly couple, the mother and at least one observer smiled with pleasure at the joy of the small one. In one small moment we were each made better because of the kindly act of a thoughtful couple.

In nursing homes many kind acts are caught as rounds are made—like seeing a new big button on the cap of a wheel chair patient. The button had large letters glaring and begging, "Help me to become all I can be." Although I did not catch the person placing the button there, one could be almost sure it was a caring son who visits his father often. They have great times together joking and laughing. One day I happened by on such a visit as Pablo burst forth in a Spanish Song—strong, beautiful from beginning to end. My reaction, "The glory of God is a person fully alive, even in his nineties." A caring son and family are bringing forth the best in Pablo.

Lord help us to learn and do likewise in each daily contact with one another. AMEN.

♡ ♡ ♡

EASTER TIDE

April 2, 1989—2nd Sunday of Easter

We are in the Easter Season, a beautiful time to be alive! All nature is awakening, and rejoicing that Christ is risen. He is alive and among us. Does our sense of awareness remind us that Christ is the Center of the Universe and that He orders all things well? **If** we look too long at the dismal happenings in our world, we fail to heal its illness. The Easter season is a good time to lift us out of lethargy and any sadness that has seeped into our lives because of existing conditions.

Here are a few suggestions to remind us that God is alive and well. We can see His Hand everywhere:

– Contemplate a crocus, a daffodil.
– Appreciate a smile and give one.
– Listen to a robin.
– Take a walk and observe new life along the way.
– Enjoy the warm sunshine.
– Rake the yard of dead leaves and think about death and resurrection.
– See the new dress or tie and say, "You look beautiful."
– If able, take an elderly person for a ride or a walk to observe Spring.
– Breathe deeply outdoors for three minutes.
– Look at the budding trees and make up a prayer.
– Bring a bit of humor to a too serious situation.

These are but a few awakeners. Do **add** to them! Rachel Carson, the good woman who warned us about spoiling our environment, had this to say in her book *Sense of Wonder*:

> "It is our misfortune that most of us have lost that clear-eyed vision, that true instinct for what is beautiful and awe-inspiring. If I had the influence with the good fairy who is supposed to preside over the Christening of all children, I should ask that her gift to each child in the world be a sense of wonder so indestructible that it would last throughout life—"

Lord, help us to see Your life in all creation and help us to recapture the wonder of childhood as we contemplate the goodness and beauty in those around us.

♡ ♡ ♡

EVANGELIZATION

August 20, 1989—20th Sunday in Ordinary Time

The Biblical School recently sponsored a presentation by Sister Martha Ann Kirk of biblical story telling and drama. For two hours

Sister related and dramatized the Exodus story and other events from Scripture. Simple costume, dance, movement, prayer and song, combined with a great love for God's Word, brought that Word to life.

She involved the audience in such a way that each person captured the message of the Word. The wanderings of the Israelites in the desert and their many trials described were reminders that we, too, are pilgrims on the way, and that the Lord is with us at each turn if we seek His guidance. "I can do all things in Him who strengthens me," St. Paul tells us.

Sister Martha Ann's presence in each movement, word and act was silent inspiration. The words of St. Iraneus came to life—"The Glory of God is a person fully alive." Sister could have achieved fame on the stage with her very special gifts of beauty and grace but she chose to Evangelize instead.

Surely many people have been encouraged to live the Gospel message of love, peace and justice through her marvelous gifts. One statement made by Sister was this: "Many people say God is dead. He is alive, but some don't know it." Her presentation of the Risen Christ and His message of hope was strong and encouraging. In closing, Sr. Martha Ann taught the audience to sing the words of Julian of Norivich, a mystic:

"All things shall be well
All things shall be well
And all manner of things shall be well."

Lord, help us to know you and the joy and the power of Your Resurrection, that we may bring others to know you better, love you more, and follow you more closely all through life. AMEN.

♡ ♡ ♡

HOPE IS ALIVE!

December 18, 1988—4th Sunday of Advent

In a small way this was revealed to me when visiting a friend who has been a semi-invalid for many years. She and her husband in failing health, had just placed luminaries on their balcony. Each year this is their way of bringing hope, joy and peace of Christmas to many people as the glowing lights cry out "Jesus comes to save us."

Another sign of hope was experienced in recalling a visit to an elderly friend in a housing project. On her door hung a picture of a bright green Christmas tree cut from a Target store ad. This lowly, beautiful adornment was but a foretaste of the hope, joy, and contentment I experienced on entering her home. What signs of hope have you experienced?

As we join with Mary in these last days of Advent, we pray that she may show us how to wait patiently as we struggle to bring the hope of Jesus born anew in us to a world in need.

"Whatever God does, the first outburst is always compassion."
—*Meister Eckhart*

♡ ♡ ♡

LENT

February 12, 1989—1st Sunday of Lent

Lent has begun—the time for giving up something.

Sean Freeman, in a book *Parables, Prayers, Psalms* gives these Twelve Suggestions.

– Give up having the last word
– Give up taking those you love for granted
– Give up worrying about things you cannot change or control
– Give up losing your temper
– Give up trying to be a perfectionist
– Give up patronizing people who work for or with you
– Give up complaining
– Give up carrying grudges

– Give up expecting to be bored by any and all sermons
– Give up nagging
– Give up thinking about money
– Give up feeling sorry for yourself

On the positive side of doing something during Lent, perhaps we can add to this list, each of which can be a prayer if done in the right spirit:

✓ Keep a secret
✓ Phone a friend
✓ Express thanks
✓ Dry an eye
✓ Sing a song in joy
✓ Warm a heart
✓ Stand up for another's rights
✓ Hug a child
✓ Laugh at yourself
✓ Plant a seed
✓ Share your bread

The reading for Ash Wednesday says:

> "Rend your hearts, return to the Lord. Goodness and merciful is He, rich in kindness. Perhaps He will again relent and leave behind Him a blessing!"

Lord, make us worthy of your blessing as we repent and change our hearts during this season of Lent. AMEN.

♡ ♡ ♡

LOVE YOUR NEIGHBOR AS YOURSELF

November 20, 1988—Christ the King

"A real friend is one who overlooks your broken down gate and admires the flowers in your window." This anonymous quotation comes from a greeting card hanging on my wall. A recent reaction to reading this was to think, "How many real friends do I have?" With ministry in mind, the answer was plain. Many of them! It would be hard to find one among my elderly friends who allows the blotches of my being to interfere with our friendship. What a blessing to see only the flowers in your friends.

I believe the acceptance and love shared by my friends is given to others also. They have learned well the message of Jesus—"Love your neighbor as yourself." *–Mark 12:31.* My tried-and-true friends fulfill this command of Jesus by accepting everyone unconditionally.

Some years ago, while struggling with this mandate of our Lord to accept and love everyone, I found some inspiration in a small book by Henri Nouwen entitled *Prayer of the Heart.* In it he speaks about the necessity of solitude in our lives if we are to have understanding and compassion for others. He relates that solitude gives birth to compassion because, as the Desert Fathers would say, it makes us die to our neighbor. What does this mean?

Fr. Nouwen explains:

> "—that in order to be of service to others we have to die to them: That is, we have to give up measuring our meaning and value with yardsticks of others. To die to our neighbors means to stop judging them, and thus, to become free, to become compassionate. Compassion can never coexist with judgment because it creates the distance, the distinction which prevents us from really being with the other."

Serious reflection on this profound thought can lead us to be the kind of Christian friends who overlook your broken down gate and admire the flowers in your window.

Lord, teach us to love our neighbor as ourselves.

♡ ♡ ♡

PEACEMAKING DAY BY DAY

May 7, 1989—7th Sunday of Easter

Pax Christi had this quote for April 23 from the Bishop's Document, *The Challenge of Peace*:

> "Let us have the courage to believe in the bright future
> And in a God who wills it for us.
> Not a perfect world, but a better one.
> Human hands and hearts and minds can create this better world."

When we listen to world and local news, we are tempted to question whether peace can be attained. Our answer must be positive and it must begin with me. Think peace, live peace, as we pray for it to happen.

Our community is working at this. Representatives of our International Congregation of Sisters—three thousand in number—will meet in October to examine present and future thrusts. As a preparation for this, we pray for these intentions daily:

- That the theme of Integrity of Creation, Justice and Peace be embraced by all of us, as a reality that be realized in our time.
- That we become more open to the many world cultures, the issues and the inter-relatedness of all people.
- That each of us may be gifted with a spirit of hope.

Let us pray for world peace:

> "Lead me from death to life, from falsehood to truth.
> Lead me from despair to hope, from fear to trust.
> Lead me from hate to love, from war to peace.
> Let peace fill our hearts, our world, our universe."

Our congregation is only one among thousands of groups, large and small, that is making special efforts for peace. And then, think of the countless individuals who are quietly making this world better. Perhaps we can add one more effort to what we are already doing.

♡ ♡ ♡

PERSEVERANCE

May 14, 1989—Pentecost Sunday

Some months ago I clipped a small news article that hit my eye and made me think. It was a statement made by a Nobel Prize winner, Joseph Brodsky, to two thousand graduates of Michigan University. He urged them never to assume the role of Victim. This is what he said.

> "No matter how abominable your condition may be, try not to blame anything or anyone—history, the state, superiors, race, parents, the phase of the moon, childhood toilet training, etc."

Brodsky, who was deported from the Soviet Union in 1972, won the Nobel Prize in Literature in 1987. No doubt he practiced what he preached.

How many times are we tempted to assume the role of victim and pass the blame for trifles or tragedies on to others. Because of our human condition, it is an easy way out.

If, on the other hand, we could spend our energy praying for guidance and brainstorming solutions, the answer would come. St. Paul said, "I can do all things in him who strengthens me." So can we, if we trust the Lord.

The following verse illustrates, in a humorous way, how two victims reacted to a situation. Take your choice:

Two frogs fell into a deep cream bowl;
  The one was wise, and a cheery soul.
The other one took a gloomy view
  And bade his friend a sad adieu.
Said the other frog with a merry grin
  "I can't get out, but I won't give in;
I'll swim around till my strength is spent,
  Then I will die the more content."
And as he swam, forever it seemed,
  His struggling began to churn the cream.
Until on top of pure butter was he

And out of the bowl he quickly hopped.
The moral, you ask? Oh, it's easily found!
If you can't get out, keep swimming around."
—*Author Unknown*

When doing God's will, never give up. Even when the going gets tough, let's keep on swimming!" —R.W.D.

We conquer by continuing. Lord, help us to keep on swimming when the waters are high.

♡ ♡ ♡

SIGN OF HOPE

March 27, 1988—Passion (Palm) Sunday

Pauline, a white haired, tranquil woman in her eighties, appears to sit comfortably in a wheel chair in her nursing home room. She often reads big print books. Her radiant smile and bright eyes light up the face of each person who comes near. Most often she is a picture of peace and contentment. If there is pain or loneliness, a visitor does not hear of it.

Pauline's tilted face, in greeting one, bears the gift of hope in all its strength. She reads lips as we exchange, "Good morning, how are you?" After apologizing for the one-hundredth time over many visits, she says, "My hearing aid doesn't work," totally innocent of the fact that no aid ever will!

My friend tells me about the book she is reading. Then she picks up a favorite prayer book from her lap and tells how she loves to pray. There are tattered leaflets extending from the well-thumbed book. A rosary is resting in her lap.

I point to a lovely framed flower painting on the wall. "I painted that," she proudly exclaims, like a child showing off it's first finger painting.

She points to another painting on the wall, describing it as if it were done that day. With pride, Pauline calls my attention to pictures of her daughter.

We then look at the gray terrier figurine on her TV set and she says, "I had several Schnauzers in Minnesota." Her smiling recollection gave one the impression that she is experiencing their live presence here and now.

It's time for Holy Communion. As I make the sign of cross and hold the pyx in my hand, Pauline folds her hands and, with reverent countenance, receives her Lord. She closes her eyes and quietly communes with Him as I ponder on leaving the room.

What a sign of hope in a suffering world!

♡ ♡ ♡

THE PRESENT MOMENT

January 15, 1989—2nd Sunday in Ordinary Time

Does it seem possible that we are half way through the first month of another year? We all no doubt experience the fast movement of time. As we do so, we may ask ourselves how we are keeping the resolution(s) we made on January first, or we might raise questions about the use and value of time that so quickly escapes us. Such reflection is good if we take time to slow down and do something about our hurried pace.

A book entitled *The Sacrament of the Present Moment*, or better known as *Self-Abandonment to Divine Providence* has a way of bringing its readers back to the importance of each moment. Pere de Caussade wrote this book in mid-1700. Its teaching is just as vital today:

> "The Sacrament of the Present Moment requires us to do our duty whatever it may be, a carrying out of God's purpose for us, not only on this day, or this hour, but this minute, this very minute—Now."

Of course this calls for attention, recollection, awareness—in order to find the treasure of each Moment. Pere de Caussade says there is no secret to finding this treasure. He states:

> "Like God, every creature whether friend or foe, pours it out generously, making it flow to the very center of our being. Divine Action cleanses the universe, pervading and flowing over all creatures."

Can we give the Lord a few quiet moments each day in which to discover this treasure, God Himself within us and around us, in every person, creature, event? With such a discovery what a power for peace our lives could be!

> "If anyone loves me he/she will keep my word and my Father will love him/her and we will come to him/her and make our home in him/her."
>
> *–John 14:23*

> "The fullness of joy is to see God in everything."
>
> *–Julian of Norwich*

♡ ♡ ♡

WELLNESS AND AGING

July 2, 1989—13th Sunday in Ordinary Time

Recently I attended a day's seminar on "Wellness and Aging—the Next Ten Years." Qualified speakers gave information on topics ranging from healthy lifestyles and preventive measures to the cost problem of health care in the future. Incidentally, one speaker predicted that Medicare would be replaced by some emerging National System of care for all by the year 1991. We'll wait and hope for that.

There was much emphasis on positive attitudes we must develop in order to take charge of our own health and not wear down the path to the doctor's office. What has this to do with the spiritual? Much! We are spiritual beings. The mind-body wellness can be a boost to the immune system and encourage efforts to promote mental-physical wellness for all. Thoughts, emotions and actions are healing factors, if positive.

One seminar speaker suggested we try these five steps to keep our immune systems working at their best:

- Create positive expectations for healing.
- Create an environment for healing with good nutrition, movement and relaxation.
- Order up large servings of love and laughter.
- Use visual imagery to speed healing, imaging the diseased area being healed.
- Appeal to the Spirit.

These items may be old stuff to us but we'll be hearing more about their value in the future. What a support we have to these measures in our faith and prayer life!

A recent study made by physicians proved the value of prayer in healing. One group of sick people was prayed for by a group of special *pray-ers*. The other group did not have prayer help. The first group healed much faster than the second group although they did not know they were being prayed for. Is not this a powerful testimony to prayer?

Healing of persons through such prayer support can surely heal a world in need. What hope for the future if we unite in healing prayer for one another and a sick world!

♡ ♡ ♡

6

God's Brat

Stories & Stuff

1993 – Time to write at an elderhostel

What you will find here is a scramble of things—all covering a diverse variety of topics and written over a wide span of years. It has been said, "Save the best for last." Whether or not I've saved the best for last, You be the judge of that!

Stories and Stuff

Story Titles in the order in which they are printed:

Abelardo
Daily Miracles
Airline Snack
Awareness
Buster's Example
Camping
Caring
Community Living at Eighty-eight
Depression
Doctor of the Poor
Doggies
Fruits of a Writing Class
Hearts Are Trumps
Humble Trust in God
Impressions of Brownie, the Chevette
Jane
Keys
Louise
Meet A Few of My Friends
Meet More of My Friends
Musings of a Minister to the Elderly
My Ticket to an Adventure
Mysterious Symphony
Name Game
Newness of Spring
Nursing Homes
Old Story - New Ending
One for the Money
Poinsettias
Quilting
Raphael
Red
Reflections on Maturity
Retreat
Shake Awake
Surprises
Symbols of Hope
The Three "R's"
Time Is a Precious Gift
Truffles
Valentine Memories
Wastebasket
Why Am I Here?

ABELARDO

It was four o'clock in the afternoon. I had just returned after a day's ministry with the elderly. As usual, a cup of coffee and the newspaper provided time to relax. It may seem strange, but one of the first pages I turn to is the funeral section. Often, I find the name of a friend who has died. At such times there is a moment of surprise and sadness followed by a gladness that comes with happy memories of my relationship with the departed.

On this recent day, the name Abelardo arose from the column. It hit me hard. I had just seen him a few days before, asleep in his bed at the nursing home. There was at once a distinct sense of loss, somewhat different from others I had experienced. Tears flowed as I reflected on our silent relationship. Suddenly, there was recollection of a little story I had written about Abelardo a few years ago. A nursing home employee wanted it for a newsletter. Immediately after finding the story, I called the mortuary for help in locating someone who could put me in touch with Aberaldo's sister in Cuba, the only survivor listed in the paper. I wanted her to have the story.

Kindly personnel at the mortuary gave me the name of a Cuban couple who had been Abelardo's faithful friends. They would be happy to translate the story and send it to his sister in Havana. I was told she was active and alert at ninety.

Because my friend was so special, here I share my story, titled *Daily Miracles*, with you. It was written in 1990 when Abelardo was losing ground. Another version of *Daily Miracles* was printed in the Fall, 1990 issue of *The Cambridge Chronicle*, the newsletter for Care-Inn at Cambridge in Lakewood, Colorado.

DAILY MIRACLES

I've been reading a book about gratefulness and prayer. It reminds me again of the importance of awareness and openness to the gift of each moment. How uplifting it is to experience the Miracle of

Awareness when we are able to ponder a smile, a flower, the song of a bird, a train whistle or the peace of inner stillness when the world around us is chaotic.

When visiting my friends on the Alzheimer's floor of a nursing home, I experience many such miracles. Each person reveals a mystery that evokes a sense of wonder, respect and gratitude for that person's life.

One such experience was given to me by Abelardo, a resident from Cuba who had been at Cambridge Care Center several years. Although he did not speak, we became good friends through smiles and handshakes. I could sense that he was a man of depth, wisdom, and goodness. With everyone, he shared a gentle courtesy and dignity that marked him as a gentleman. Abelardo appreciated religious services and responded pleasantly to a sign of the cross or other religious symbols.

Some months ago, Abelardo withdrew and lost contact with those around him. Communication was nil until Ray, a kind orderly, placed a sign on his door saying, "Abelardo likes hugs." And so it was. Caretakers heeded the sign, and his happy smile returned.

One day, on my usual rounds, I found Abelardo dozing in a comfortable chair in the lounge. His small body, with a bushy white head, closed eyes and wrinkled face, rested comfortably. He was a man at peace.

While wondering if I should call my friend by name, it occurred to me that a gentle back massage might rouse him. It worked. An unusual surprise awaited me. After a few brief moments, Abelardo slowly lifted his bushy head, looked at me, and beamed his happy smile of recognition. We sat silently for a few moments. Then his hand slowly reached up to take my hand. Ever so gently he placed it between his palms and rested them in his lap while gazing into the distance. At this moment, it was as if God had touched my hand and all of me. It was a sacred experience.

Lowering his eyes as if pondering his next move, Abelardo gently placed my hand in my lap. Slowly and thoughtfully he stood up and walked ever so softly to a near-by table. With great dignity and caution, he clasped the chair and placed it under the table. Then he began his usual duties of smoothing the cloth of any wrinkles and carefully arranging the service. You see, Abelardo had been a waiter in a fine restaurant in Cuba.

~ ~ ~ ~ ~ ~ ~

AIRLINE SNACK

Trip home from Phoenix to Denver on Flight 218
February, 1991

Small boxes are piled high on a cart. A uniformed hostess rearranges each on her firm body shelf—her arm. Smiling, she distributes her noonday refreshment. No passenger is too engrossed in book, magazine or conversation to ignore this simple meal or, more than that, the pleasant words and smile of a gracious hostess.

The beverage to follow is dispensed with the same courtesy, "—to serve you is a pleasure," only this time by a tall, friendly male host. Passengers respond with relaxed satisfaction.

Back to the box, the small container had a peep-through window revealing a child-size apple, a bag of goldfish cheese snacks, and crackers in cellophane. Lifting the box lid brings more surprises: a bite-size cheese pack and cookie wrapped transparently, all neatly reposing in their made-to-fit dwelling. Glancing around, I observe the first choice selection of sister and brother passengers. Mine is cheese and crackers, but I must work for the morsel. My small cracker pack calls for a teething exercise on a stubborn wrapper. The cheese pack requires less labor. A small protruding string says pull me. I do so as soft cheese bulges out to mess my hands. A quick finger bowl from a chunk of ice does the trick, and I am ready for lunch.

Yes, this is a small feast to enjoy as one rides homeward, reflecting on a joy filled week with family in the Land of the Sun.

~ ~ ~ ~ ~ ~ ~

AWARENESS

To find beauty where one normally would not see it, requires a special gift—awareness. This gift can be innate for some. Others can develop or recapture this gift with a bit of effort.

Most children have an innate sense of awareness. They immediately see the beauty, goodness, and essence of a flower, a puppy dog, a cartoon on TV, their mother's cooking, grandma's smile, and a friend's greeting. To each person or thing, a child is generally present to the moment unless distracted by people-made situations.

We adults look with a certain envy at children's unconscious delight and enjoyment of the ordinary. Rachel Carson, in her book, *Sense of Wonder*, has this to say:

> "A child's world is fresh and new and beautiful, full of wonder and excitement. It is our misfortune that, for most of us, that clear-eyed vision, that true instinct for what is beautiful and awe-inspiring, is dimmed and even lost before we reach adulthood. If I had the influence with the good fairy, who is supposed to preside over the christening of all children, I should ask that her gift to each child in the world be a sense of wonder, so indestructible that it would last throughout life, as an unfailing antidote against the boredom and disenchantment of later years, the sterile preoccupation with things that are artificial, the alienation from the sources of our strength."

How can we adults regain the child in us and rediscover with one the joy, excitement, and mystery of the world we live in but do not always see?

Perhaps we need to remove from our cluttered memories the debris collected through too much TV, newspaper, superficial reading, meaningless conversations, and noise. How can we return to the center of our being that has become so obscured by these distractions?

The answer is simple. Slow down, seek solitude, find time to be alone. Such periods of silence are bound to quiet the soul and re-open its eyes to the world around us. Our feelings and emotions, cleansed of noisy distractions, can more readily see the new, the beautiful and the mysterious, that abounds everywhere in nature and humankind.

~ ~ ~ ~ ~ ~ ~

BUSTER'S EXAMPLE

1980s

Bringing Holy Communion to members of nursing home residents and shut-ins over a ten year ministry is a rewarding experience. However, it happens from time to time, that I am thoughtless and unmindful of the beautiful mystery of the Eucharist, a precious gift carried on my person.

This fact was revealed to me in a special way recently while helping Sr. Rose, our Mother of the Poor, with whom I shopped weekly before Thanksgiving to purchase food for baskets. On one Saturday, the bakery-lady-in-charge gave Sister two large shopping carts full of bread and topped it with a reverent hug, all a precious gift for the needy. As I rolled the carts to the car, a young man came with me to transfer the bread. I started tossing the loaves into the trunk of the car. Buster, as he was known to Sr. Rose, lifted each loaf gently and placed it reverently in a neat row. Quickly, I caught his example and did likewise until the bread was neatly arranged and stacked. During this time, my reflections were on gentleness and reverence, and Eucharistic Bread.

I thanked Buster for sharing his care for God's poor and remarked, "If you can always reverence people as I've observed your handling of this bread, you'll be a big success in life." He smiled.

That simple example of a caring grocery boy revealed to me, not only the call to reverence all of God's creatures, but it was also a strong reminder, above all, to be mindful and reverent with the Bread of Life, Christ Himself, at all times.

~ ~ ~ ~ ~ ~ ~

CAMPING

Camping is for the young, or so it may have been at one time. It is good to hear of a grandmother enjoying such a weekend with grandchildren. Marje is an example of the aliveness, seeing and doing what can be done and enjoying it all.

With her cheerful, outgoing personality that is centered on others, I can visualize her singing with gusto around a campfire with the young and adventurous.

If the day or a long hike should become monotonous, I can hear her enlivening it with a story or pointing out creatures of interest along the way, whether it be grass, flowers, insects, or the sky.

Meals? I'll bet Marje comes prepared with her best outdoor recipes and plenty of hot dogs and marshmallows.

~ ~ ~ ~ ~ ~ ~

CARING

1980s

The month of May is an exciting month in many ways. It brings Mother's Day, May crowning, May baskets, proms, graduations, and parties. One of the lesser-known events is Nursing Home Week—May twelfth through eighteenth this year. It is not on the popularity ladder but each year it climbs a step higher. Devoted personnel, volunteers and agencies work tirelessly to interest the public in this event. Nursing homes will celebrate with extra activities and entertainment. Residents are made to feel at home through this special gift of caring.

Care givers in nursing homes work long hours to bring loving attention to its residents. They find it rewarding to see family, friends and volunteers show that they too care by their visits, phone calls, letters, cards, gifts—especially on bleak, ordinary days.

Through many years of pastoral ministry in nursing homes, I look back with gratitude for relationships with my elderly friends. They have enfleshed the meaning of faith, love, wisdom and other beautiful gifts. Those who work in any way with the elderly would probably agree that it is a mutual ministry. The scales are tipped in favor of the minister or visitor.

My learning experiences began when I started visiting nursing homes many years ago. My mission was to represent the Church in bringing the Gospel message to people who could no longer attend church services. Efforts were made to provide symbols of the past in these devotions. Residents respond well to traditional practices. In addition to arranging services, I felt called to bring something else to my friends. However, there was some uncertainty as to what that something was! There were times when I went to bat for some residents. These efforts ranged from reporting odors and soiled linens to crusading for cookies to treat my friends.

In a short time I learned that sometimes complaints bring one to a dead end, and the brick wall can be hard! As for treats, it was found that my good people liked cookies, but they were looking more for the human touch of one who cares. Cookies were like band-aids. The message was strong. Something to bring was oneself, one who listens and cares. The lesson is an ongoing learning experience for anyone sharing with the elderly.

For many people, the words "nursing home" are still a dreaded sound, and they bring forth a storm of stereotypes. For others, the picture has become brighter, more hopeful—they look and they **see** improved care. My experience shows the latter to be true.

In general, patients are happier and more content in a nursing home. After initial adjustments, many feel it is their home. They speak about care received.

Citizens and agencies continue to do something constructive about changes needed to meet State standards. Today one can find policies, residence rights, minutes of resident-staff meetings, and other reports listed on bulletin boards, or in newsletters for the public to read.

Residents meet regularly with staff members for open discussions. Their comments range from complaints about room temperatures to selecting menus for special days. The minutes record the sublime and the humorous.

Cleanliness makes headlines. Housekeepers and janitors serve with pride. They share joy and humor with residents as they make their rounds.

There are more varied activities for entertainment and participation. These range from current events and spelling bees to spring proms, including formal dress and escorts. There are Special Olympics, walk-a-thons and wheelchair events.

Decor and furnishings are in good taste. Residence rooms often show family care with photos, flowers and memories of the past.

Active elderly are free to complain and receive attention. Employees try to keep an extra eye on those confined to bed. Visitors may report a resident's needs.

A caring attitude among personnel including administrators continues to grow. Nurses aides are very special. Wages are hardly the motive because they are minimally paid. Some homes retain employees for a longer period of time—a good sign.

Hair care and manicures as well as barber and beauty shop visits visibly boost the self confidence and sense of dignity in the resident.

Churches, schools, groups and individuals provide Christmas gifts and treats on special days. Children bring homemade cards and gifts, sing songs and give hugs. Some even adopt a home for long-range caring.

Volunteers perform services for the elderly by visiting with them, playing games, reading, letter writing.

Churches have regular services. These provide food for the spirit and companionship as they worship God together.

The list could go on—all of which adds up to caring. Nursing home status is not perfect, but it is greatly improved.

A longtime friend, Thelma, who turned ninety recently, sent me a book of her own writings. Each one is a treasure. One poem sums up the life and experience of the elderly:

The Stub

The roots went deep for needed strength.
Its trunk grew straight through blasting winds.
The branches spread in beauty green.
Still it grew til shoulder to shoulder with its peers.
Its head was held high. Strong it stood.
Then ice storms struck its branches down.
Lightning struck its bark away.
It's white wood bared.
Still firm it stands, unbeaten,
Holding it's own through time,
A statue to integrity!

—Thelma Barrett

Some aged person somewhere is waiting for our love and care. For anyone interested in visiting the elderly or who wishes to find meaning in life, there is an answer. Contact the activities director in a nursing home and be a friend to a lonely resident. You'll find a new true friend if you bring your caring self.

~ ~ ~ ~ ~ ~ ~

COMMUNITY LIVING AT EIGHTY-EIGHT

Written for the Midwest Chronicle, newsletter for the Sisters of St. Francis
Sacred Heart Province, Denver, Colorado
December, 2006 - edited January, 2007

Early in the novitiate, one of the strangest statements I heard was made by Mother Lidwina in talking to us about relationships. She said, "Community living does not get easier with age." Yes, to me that was hard to believe. We were such a happy bunch. Now after seventy-two years of community living, I can understand the wisdom of that statement.

We here at Marian are a motley group of oldies ranging in ages from sixty to ninety-eight. Our ailments are varied, as one would find in any nursing home. If our combined IQs could be averaged, the final number would probably shout, "Smart bunch!" And if all our accomplishments were added up, they'd make a sizable pile.

How is such a group doing as Community in this year 2006? I ask myself that question, pondering it for some time. The answer is loud and clear. We are a struggling, praying Community. I'd like to say loving Community but that doesn't sound right. We are trying to be. The dictionary defines struggle in this way: "to make strenuous efforts against opposition; to proceed with great effort; an act of strongly motivated striving." Now, that's us!

Another bit of wisdom I picked up somewhere was, "Don't expect anything and you'll never be disappointed." Aware of one another's weaknesses, we try hard to respect the dignity of each one. I'm sure that each and all of us end our morning meditation on a note such as this: "Lord, help me to touch another with my love this day." We try! Good Mother Teresa gave us the simple wisdom, "We can do no great thing, only small things, with great love." And so it is, with great gratitude, that we experience small surprises from time to time.

Our surprises are as diverse as we are as individuals. Here are a few:

- To get a wheelchair push when my arms are weary.
- Information on any topic needed or meaning of a word.
- Making the adjustment to walker or wheelchair cheerfully.

♥ Sharing the Register or doing an act of charity when there's a need.
♥ Sharing one's jolly self after a day's work.
♥ Finding a tattered Bible with a new cover, after it had disappeared for two days.
♥ Putting my file in good order after receiving equipment brought from Marycrest.
♥ Watching the fish in two aquariums rush toward Sister as she brings their daily food.
♥ Hearing about one Sister's condition through another Sister who brings her Holy Communion regularly.
♥ Surprises arrive daily in the mailbox, from 1st–4th class.
♥ Knowing the needy are being helped through funds made available through the Ministerial Association.
♥ Sharing the weekly *Commonweal* and any information on movements in the church.
♥ To witness one Sister's prayerfulness and patience with near blindness.
♥ To receive *America* weekly and sometimes finding a new book for sharing.
♥ I'm happy if I can bring one Sister a cup of coffee and read a letter to another.

Yes, we are a struggling, praying community. I close with this prayer:

Lord, open our eyes to see the little needs around us,
to know when another needs a word or touch,
to overlook human weaknesses,
to forget my own wants and search for ways to help another,
to be prayerful and grateful—always with great love.
Yes, Lord, help us to keep struggling and striving
to be a Community of Love. Amen

~ ~ ~ ~ ~ ~ ~

DEPRESSION

Dark, dismal days demand patient endurance as the demons of darkness have their day. I pray, but God seems far away. Efforts to be cheerful, to be OK, to do things in a normal way, are put-ons, not the real. I sense the cause is too much **me**. On desert time I need to feed.

There in silence, but for inner urges, I hear God's message through poet, Jessica Powers. She lets me know, from her own ways, that God is good and wants my all, not just half. Lord, accept my desires to be cheerful, to be okay, to do things in a normal way, and let them become a reality, if You will.

~ ~ ~ ~ ~ ~ ~

DOCTOR OF THE POOR

2006

A stop at the church office brought a surprise one day in 1983, when Helen, the secretary, told me there had been a call from a woman who wanted to do volunteer work. That was good news! I lost no time in searching for the note with her telephone number.

In a few days, Joyce, a lady in her forty's, appeared ready for service. To the nursing home we went, as she told me about herself. She was here for a few months to help her family. She was working in Brazil and would be returning there in a few months.

It was plain to see that Joyce was a people person who gave caring attention to each person she met. On second or third rounds, Joyce told me that she was a doctor and worked with Sr. Dulce, the Mother Teresa of Brazil, who managed a hospital for the poorest of the poor in Bahia, a most arid region in mid-eastern Brazil.

As we became friends, Joyce shared her story. She came into the church at seventeen, the only Catholic in her family. After her graduation from college, she had a stint in the Peace Corps that led her to work with the poor in Northern Brazil. Having experienced the extreme poverty there, she made up her mind to become a doctor.

Back in Denver, she received her MD and Doctor of Surgery. Returning to Brazil, she was led to Sr. Dulce's hospital for the poorest of the poor in San Salvador, Bahia.

Joyce's sharing of her story evoked my deep admiration for this dedicated woman. After seven months in Denver, Joyce returned to Brazil, leaving many nursing home residents and home bound to miss her joy-filled visits.

Sadly, after one year back in her devoted ministry, Dr. Joyce was diagnosed with incurable cancer. She came home to her beloved brother and family to prepare for death. They and her extended family gave her the most loving care.

In all those months of painful suffering, Joyce showed the utmost optimism and hope, right up to the day of death, just as she had lived every day of her life. It was a special gift to witness her deep faith.

In the Sisters Section of Calvary Cemetery in Denver there is a headstone on a grave, in one corner, which reads:

JOYCE DeMILLE—Doctor of the Poor—1938-1985

Dr. Joyce had wanted to be a Religious, but it was not her calling. She gave to God and the Church her very best as a lay woman.

Although she in **no way** intimated this, we, who got to know Joyce, had expected her to head the hospital in Brazil as Sister Dulce's health was failing. Her death was a tragic loss for the poor.

~ ~ ~ ~ ~ ~ ~

DOGGIES

1990s

Occasionally, I house sit and doggie sit for a friend's two poodles, Prince and Rosie. Prince is white and small, the first to find a home with Betty, a marathon runner. Rosie arrived a few years later. Also, Rosie is a bit longer and darker than Prince. They have become great friends but do not lean on each other. At one time, Rosie was a bit domineering, but Prince reacted by ignoring it and maintaining her own peace and independence. Rosie soon lost her pushiness. Both dogs play well together and on occasion can be playfully scrappy.

When one sleeps, the other sleeps. At meal time, both enjoy what is set before them, sometimes snacking from the other's dish. When it's time to bring in the mail, both like to receive a piece of junk mail. Proudly they carry it between their teeth from mailbox to house.

One thing no one has been able to figure out is the barking furor that erupts when the mailman approaches in his white truck. Prince had always been aggressive, bouncing and barking as the mail truck approached at the mailbox. Rosie picked up on this and just as loudly gives the mailman a barking message.

Prince is gentle, sensible and mature. Rosie is bouncy and playful while, at times, showing the need to grow up. An example—I wear a hearing aid that is placed on the night stand at night. One morning, I missed the aid and began a search. It was nowhere to be found. Because the doggies sleep on top at the foot of the bed, I suspected Rosie. She does become restless at times. Returning to the room, I looked over the situation again. Picking up a small folded blanket at the foot of the bed, there was the evidence. Rosie had found the aid, thinking it a bone, and chewed parts of the plastic and tubing into a neat little pile, and then hid her bones under the blanket.

Aside from this incident, there are no complaints about the doggies. I fully appreciate Prince and Rosie and look forward to sitting with my friends.

Postscript: September, 2006 Today I received a photograph of these two poodles with their "Mom" Betty holding them. This message was on the reverse of the photo:

> "Dear Sr. Kathryn, Thank you for the many times you took care of us, and for the peace of mind you gave to Betty during her marathon adventures. We love you. Please keep us in your memory. God bless you." /s/ Princey, Rosie and Betty

A letter explained that both poodles died within three months of each other this past year. Pepe and Kate are new puppies to take their place. What fond memories Betty's letter and photo invoked!

Princey
Betty
Rosie

~ ~ ~ ~ ~ ~ ~

'FRUITS' OF A WRITING CLASS

We were to select a topic,
"cluster" our thoughts,
then write a short paragraph or story about them.

BLIZZARD

Winter in Colorado can be interesting and stimulating. It brings with it the threat of unexpected blizzards, the challenge of survival, the opportunity for winter sports fun and the call to meditate with joy on the beauty it provides.

LETTING GO

Letting go can be a difficult process for one to undergo. It makes demands on me that can be threatening and painful to my ego. Circumstances and relationships that call forth the letting go process can be a hidden blessing. The act of letting go, of abandoning my self-centeredness, can be painful. The conquest, when made, is itself the reward. Personal freedom is gained, and an unhealthy self experiences healing.

AIRPLANE

My first ride in an airplane was preceded by apprehension, fear and down right dread. Having heard stories from childhood about a plane crash, in which the Savidge Brothers were killed, instilled a certain fear of the flying machine.

Knowing that these brothers had invented their own machine and were quite respected in the limited aviation area of Deloit, Nebraska, did not change those fears. Somehow all airplanes were dangerous.

These were probably among my varied and anxious thoughts as I boarded my first plane—not a short trip mind you—but to Rome, the Eternal City. The stewardess listened to my uneasiness as I stated, "This is my first plane ride." She sat beside me until we were safely in the air and my fears changed to total enjoyment.

FEAR

Fear was my enemy in early childhood and as I grew up. My earliest recollection was fear of the dark. Seldom could I be left alone after darkness set in. The cause of this was a mystery and assurances from my family that "there's nothing in the dark" did not help. Furthermore, their innocent laughing at my fears of darkness and things that didn't happen only made matters worse. My mother's assurance would be a temporary comfort. Some of my fears bordered on phobias. Tornado, blizzard, the house burning down, having to mortgage our farm, money needs, the cream check not covering the grocery bill, running out of something, my mother getting sick and dying, that drouth would put us on the county, farm accidents, and numberless other imagined situations caused me constant instant fear. Among the greatest fears, however, was my fear of God Himself. It was hard to relate to Him as a loving Father. Images of the stern, white-bearded God evoked fear of His judgement and punishment. The best part of my life emerged years ago when I began to realize and accept the fact that God is a loving Father and not out to get us. Self-forgetfulness helps to conquer fear. Jesus said, "Perfect love casts out fear." Today, in my late seventies, I thank God sincerely for continued healing and deliverance from the numerous fears that bound me and made me un-free. Such freedom evokes the prayer, "Give thanks to the Lord for He is good. His mercy is forever."

WHITE

White is the absence of color, a gift that brings life and joy to each day. White! The absence of this precious gift can bring its own special meaning to us in various ways. The white letter in the mail can certainly brighten our day. A small red heart or bright flower seal does not detract, but enhances, the white and adds to its beauty. The woman or man in a fresh white blouse or shirt commands a certain respect. The white garment can speak of uniqueness, freshness, reserve, respect. Again, a bit of color in the tie can add interest as it does to any white garment. White sheets, on the other hand, can give the feeling of confinement, lack of cheer. I prefer to sleep among the flowers. White speaks of purity, freedom from the dust, dirt and grime of the world whether it be from the earth itself or from the abuse of morality. We are reminded of the purity of the Mother of God. One poet called her Tainted Nature's Solitary Boast.

PEOPLE

Barbara, you are learning patience and you are teaching me the same by clinging to your goals.

Our concerns are so much alike—love for the poor, the rejected, the oppressed and suffering people of the world.

Your goal, to help people help themselves, is an ideal. Your newly gained degree in the right field will enable you to do this, but now the disappointment of not getting a job in that field! Barb, I try to practice patience along with you. If prayer had an instant answer, you'd have had a job long ago. In the meantime, you are experiencing patience and discipline through the lowly task of housecleaning. Courage, Barb, the right Community Organizing job is out there with your name on it!

Postscript: 2006 Today Barb is using her degree in Community Organization. In San Francisco's Tenderloin area, she helped many people to solve their housing problems. She continues this work now with Mercy Housing.

~ ~ ~ ~ ~ ~ ~

HEARTS ARE TRUMPS

written for and printed in a Nursing Home newsletter
1988

Josephine, a long-time resident of a nursing home where I minister, died recently at the age of ninety-nine. She was gentle and soft spoken but unyielding in her persistence to live. Josephine became a friend to many. At her passing, the patients who knew her well shared their grief and stories.

Some years ago, Josephine's husband, Casimir, took up residence in the same nursing home. Because they were in rooms at the opposite ends of the hall, I presumed that relations between them had not been too good.

Casimir was outspoken and at times appeared to be downright crabby. Never did he appear at our religious services until shortly before his death—another reason for me to think that their marriage was not a happy one.

One day when speaking to a daughter about his un-churchiness, she assured me that her father was a good man who did not wear his religion on his sleeve, that Casimir had a warm heart under the rough surface and was a highly respected man.

His family understood that and loved him. Having been told that he was a Union leader for years explained it all. Another interesting fact I learned was that Josephine was the strong one in the marriage. Male chauvinism had no place in their life, I was told.

One of the stories related by a staff member after Josephine's passing came as a surprise to me. A nurse recalled seeing Josephine wheel her husband down the corridor to his room one day as an elderly man approached. He remarked, "My Josephine, you look good today," and walked on by.

Casimir, ever on the alert, snapped, "Get in this room and stay here!" Indeed, I had to eat my thoughts about their unhappy marriage.

~ ~ ~ ~ ~ ~ ~

HUMBLE TRUST IN GOD

Reflections on Psalm 131

on a Saturday morning during a quiet mountain retreat

O lord, my heart is not proud.

As I glance toward mountains eastward, my eyes turn to moving figures in a yard across the road.

Nor are my eyes haughty.

A father and small child step outside from their home. He lays small rugs on the ground, then lifts the small blonde girl on his strong shoulders and off they go for a short walk in the woods.

I busy not myself with great things
nor things too sublime for me.

This is indeed grace. Father returns, gently lowers child to ground and sweeps the rugs while child and retreatant reflect on father's brisk but gentle strokes. After each rug is swept the little girl steps on each one, imprinting the stamp of a father's love on family carpets.

Nay, rather, I have stilled and quieted my soul,
like a weaned child, so is my soul within me.

Father takes one rug at a time into the house while helpful child with tiny broom sweeps the door step to a loving home. Father then emerges again and takes child into his arms for another walk in the woods.

Like a weaned child on its mother's lap,
on it's father's shoulders,
in his strong arms,
so is my soul within me.

What a gift of love you have provided, my God, a vision to provide even greater growth in our Father's love.

O, Israel, hope in the Lord,
both now and forever.

Family love is alive and well for many. Others need it. Lord, make it so for them. Thank you for Your loving care of us. Amen

~ ~ ~ ~ ~ ~ ~

IMPRESSIONS OF Brownie, THE CHEVETTE

the Parish car I use for my work with the elderly
February 5, 1985

☆ A brown car is a fortuitous gift because it is the color symbol of my Franciscan family.

☆ I feel proud and fortunate to be able to slither into small spaces not made for the biggies.

☆ My car is a trustful companion as I bring joy and friendliness to people.

☆ Brownie is humble, unassuming, the mark of a good Franciscan.

☆ My confidence is increased on cold mornings because of Brownie's ability to start promptly.

☆ As I drive, I feel comfortable in singing off key, or shouting frustrations at times, because Brownie is a safe listener.

☆ I learn patience as I wait at stop signs or move slowly up hill waiting for the Chevette to slowly get in gear.

☆ I am challenged to trust at times when I feel insecure, knowing the car is vulnerable to powerful vehicles that pass.

☆ The Chevette reminds me of the book *Small is Beautiful.*

☆ Brownie is a gas-saver which pleases my thrifty nature.

I am developing a good relationship with Brownie through writing this.

Postscript: 2006 I used this car for several years. Whatever happened to Brownie, I do not remember.

~ ~ ~ ~ ~ ~ ~

JANE

February, 1985 - rev. 2006

On the afternoon of February twelfth, 1985, I picked up a written telephone message when I return from work. The note read, "Jane is back in the hospital and is calling for you." I immediately called the hospital in Nebraska. Jane could not talk, but her husband relayed my message of concern and prayer. He said she would be going home in a few days.

Jane had been diagnosed two months earlier as having cancer of the pancreas, a very painful form of cancer. Jane did not need this, I thought as I had read the news written by Sr. Clarice from the hospital in December, 1984. My heart ached for her as I recalled the hard life she had.

The news brought back many memories of Jane and her family. She and her family were neighbors who lived on a forty-acre farm adjoining our small farm in the sandhills of Nebraska.

As I drove to work the next day, memory after memory flashed through my mind as I moved west on I-Seventy. The first pictures that came to mind was that of Jane and myself trudging down the dirt road after our one-room school closed for the afternoon on Valentine's Day in the late 1920s. She was about eleven and I was a little younger. Our homes were in the same direction so Jane and I, my little sister Ann, my older brother Bill, and Jane's two brothers sometimes walked together 'til we got to the meadow. From there Ann and I cut across to save time and steps.

That particular day we drew valentines out of the usual decorated exchange box. The valentines ranged from cute little five-for-a-penny hearts with silly sayings to homemade hearts decorated with black and white pictures of animals or birds from the Nebraska farm magazine or colorful pictures of well-dressed people from the Sears Roebuck catalog. My valentine from Jane was a new Christmas postcard with a picture of Santa on the front. On the reverse—"to Catherine from Jane." A few other children received similar cards and there were a few snickers which I hoped Jane and her brothers had not noticed.

I recall small talk as we walked the road home that day. I wanted to thank Jane for her card, but was fearful of embarrassing her. I remember saying something like, "Jane, I liked your card", and I can still hear her say, "They're just as good as valentines."

And so they were. New cards, red in color, they were given with care though Christmas was the theme. And why not celebrate Christmas any and every day? Is it not the feast of love?

I recall my feelings of compassion for Jane and her family who were battling the depression, just as we were. These same feelings were with me now, as I drove on thinking of Jane in her present painful illness.

I recall that the she and her brothers were absent from school quite often. Work at home, improper clothing, lack of decent food for the dinner bucket, any number of things may have been the cause. It became an accepted fact that the family did what they could, and omitted what they could not, for whatever reason.

Jane's family consisted of parents—Pauline and The Old Man. I honestly cannot recall her father's first name—and five brothers—four them at home, one younger and three older—all living in a dwelling of three small rooms, a typical farm dwelling, with kerosene lamp, an outdoor water pump and an outhouse. On occasional visits, we'd peek into the kitchen which had an old kitchen range with wood box next to it, a dish cupboard and a small table. In the corner was a cot where The Old Man rested.

Three things I recall about Jane's father: he was mean; he drank bootleg whiskey—my brother said you could find a tan and brown earthenware jug under the cot at any time, but I doubt if he ever got that close—and thirdly, The Old Man was never seen in the fields or barnyard. The boys and their mother, with Jane, did the farm work.

The Old Man's meanness was impressed on my memory as I still can recall one hot summer afternoon when my little sister, Ann, and I— about seven and eight at the time— ventured over to visit Jane. We did so with fear and trembling, and some curiosity, plus the fact that our widowed mother always wanted us to be friendly. The family had two lean, coyote-looking dogs which would start barking madly when anyone crossed the barb wire fence separating our farms. Over a period of time we did learn that the dogs bark was worse than their bite, which we never actually experienced.

That hot afternoon we got past the dogs and approached the house. We heard curses and shouting as we stood still on the sandy, curved path that led to the house. There stood Pete, youngest son, about five or six years of age. He was dancing up and down in bare feet in the hot sand screaming as The Old Man switched the small boy's naked legs with a long willow switch. His overalls were rolled above his knees, probably in obedience to The Old Man's order. The little boy cried loudly as my sister and I stood there, sad and helpless.

If I recall correctly, I think we turned and went home where we told our mother the story. She, too, was sad for she cared for this family.

My mother was Jane's godmother in baptism so she tried to give her special attention when there was contact. Jane appreciated this kindness. At Christmas, gifts were scarce in those depression years, but my mother always had something for Jane's family. Jane could count on one special thing from my mother, as could the six of us.

As time moved on, I went to high school and then entered the convent in New York State in 1931. Jane remained at home milking the cows, feeding chickens, and often doing heavier farm work.

A few years after I was in the convent—sometime in the early 1940s—I received a letter from my sister, Teck, which had this major news, "Jane eloped with a hired man. He and Jane came to use our phone. He called his parents in eastern Nebraska to tell them he was bringing Jane home with him. Mom says it's the only way Jane can get away from the place." I was both surprised and relieved, and hoped life would be better for Jane.

For years, there was no contact, even with her own family. Then, about ten years ago, our family learned that Jane had moved to a farm in another area of Nebraska. I got her name and address and we've exchanged Christmas cards and an occasional letter since then.

Her letters were short. One told that she had to do hard work whilehe didn't do much of anything. Another letter told of nearly going crazy because her granddaughter had a baby and was living with them. Then one year they sold everything and moved to a small town. The letter that followed related how there was nothin' to do. Yes, life was not easy for Jane. In between the hard times, I hope there were many unrecorded happy times.

Each day, now, I hope and pray that Jane will experience the healing love of Jesus as she prepares to enter into a better life where there is no more pain and sorrow.

Postscript: 2007 Jane died peacefully at home. Her family and hospice had cared for her there. I am now in touch with her daughter. One of Jane's brothers went east and did well. Three of the boys stayed on the farm. The last survivor left a sizable amount of money to St. Peter's Church in Ewing which helped pay for a renovation and new paint.

~ ~ ~ ~ ~ ~ ~

KEYS

Keys are important instruments of safety and freedom. A key gives us entrance to our home and makes it safe when we leave. For personal items in a suit case, box or cupboard, a key can give one freedom from worry about valuable belongings.

Keys to the car, whether for the ignition or trunk, are very important. The loss of one or another can cause great inconvenience, worry, even panic, if not found within a reasonable length of time. The same holds for keys to homes, business or other buildings.

I am reminded of an old prayer book, *Key to Heaven*. It might be considered an heirloom at this time, unless some remote publisher considers it important for the older generation. The book might be out of print, but the title is ever timely. Prayer will always be the Key to Heaven no matter how we pray—silently without a book, meditation on Scripture, sharing verbally in a group, saying the rosary, attending Mass, reflecting on nature.

On a down day, the sun's rays coming through a window can lighten one's spirits, can prompt a grateful prayer, a Key to Heaven that transforms. A child's smile or happy chatter can lift us on high—still another Key to Heaven.

And so it goes, around the clock. Prayer is the key that keeps us in touch with ourselves and God Himself. Lord, let us always keep the Key to Heaven safe and handy!

~ ~ ~ ~ ~ ~ ~

LOUISE

1980s

Louise is over seventy, brown skinned, small in stature, wiry. We've been friends a long time. We met through a telephone call she placed at the church asking for Holy Communion to be brought to her. Louise lives with her son in a rented house near a Catholic hospital where she sometimes is able to walk to Sunday Mass.

Getting to know Louise was not easy. I was not sure of her real needs and, in trying to be friendly, talked about various and sundry things. Louise, a Native American Sioux Indian, was all the time sizing me up and one day blurted out, "Be yourself!" That remark of course, made me think. Through more visits, and as time passed, she helped me to be myself, which brought about our friendship.

Louise is quite self-sufficient, but she accepts my small gifts of fruit, cookies or flowers with gratitude. What she really needs is someone she can chat with, and that we do.

One day she was making a quilt top for a small boy, a friend of hers. The crisp blue denim squares were all cut, and bright red designs were being readied to sew on the squares. Each piece is evenly cut and pressed. On succeeding visits I was to see the finished quilt top, a perfect work of art. What impressed me most during the progress of this project was her love and concern for the little boy. Her eyes and sparkle along with a smile, as she'd exclaim, "Won't this make him happy!" or, "I can hardly wait to see him when he sees the quilt."

Louise loved to cook and she canned vegetables and fruit when they were in season. One day she invited me to her cupboard. What an array of jars, all in rows, some pint size, others quart. There were beets, carrots, tomatoes, peaches, and other varieties I cannot recall. Louise was rightfully proud of her handiwork.

This year there will be no canning. Louise has had cancer surgery and is slowly regaining strength. During the series of radiation treatments, she would speak of the long waits for treatment and the long rides to and from the University Hospital in the vehicle used to transport those in need of such. Always her description of the waits and the trips were touched with a bit of humor. Underneath it all I could detect a valiant, faith-filled Louise accepting a heavy burden of illness and trying to make the best of it.

Postscript: 2007 Louise died and left a grieving son who had lived with her.

~ ~ ~ ~ ~ ~ ~

MEET A FEW OF MY FRIENDS

1987 - 1988

Each of the following vignettes is only a glimpse into the lives of some whom I serve in my Parish Ministry.

Agnes likes to receive Holy Communion. She sits in her nursing home room with an afghan covering her body and keeps repeating, "I'm sick, I'm sick." I assure her that Jesus heals and give her the Sacrament. She becomes more peaceful as we pray. Several times I've met loving daughters who visit their mother faithfully. Agnes' husband, whose age is in the high nineties, is doing well in his own home.

Ann, at eighty-three, is still able to be in her own home, which she dearly loves. Arthritis makes ambulation wobbly at times, but Ann's persistence enables her to do all her own work. Even the flowers and weeds feel her gentle or not so gentle touch. Anne's favorite place is her prayer corner, where she spends a lot of time sitting in her deceased husband's favorite chair. A stack of well-thumbed books and leaflets nearby testify to her devotion to her Lord and His friends. Surely her faithfulness to prayer accounts for her courageous attitude to face each day.

Genevieve is a staunch Catholic and regrets that we can't have mass more often in the nursing home. She received her education in the Convent of the Good Shepherd and once told me, "When it was time for us to leave, the sisters did not want to let us go, they loved us so much." Such memories are a comfort to her now. The death of a son several months ago brought grief, but Genevieve surmounts her loss with deep faith and trust in the Lord.

George is ninety-six and failing. For several years after coming to the nursing home, he sang *How Great Thou Art* at every Catholic service. George is proud of the fact that he had sung in the church choir for seventeen years. The past few months his voice is silent, but he attributes this failure to the acoustics which are unable to carry his voice.

Gloria is a beautiful retarded lady who has been in a semi-coma the past two years of the six years she has been in a nursing home. Before she lost contact, Gloria greeted everyone who came her way with a big smile and outstretched arms. Always, she received Holy Communion knowingly and reverently. Hers was a loving mother and family of deep faith who cared for her at home, until her mother had to go to the hospital with cancer. Gloria was fifty-one then.

John is blind and must be led to and from our service. He carefully follows the handrail while clasping his guide's hand. John is a courteous gentleman, always giving a gentle thank you for each bit of help. He follows the service reverently with moving lips. During the day he sometimes sits in the lounge, holding hands with a friend. In silence, he communes with his God and his friends.

Mary is an elderly mental patient who spends her time walking the halls silently in a nursing home. Even when she lost a sister in the home not long ago, Mary did not speak. When we meet, she smiles and we hug each other. The sign of the cross and appearance of the pyx bring forth another smile. After receiving Holy Communion, Mary continues her walk and the Lord walks in her.

Pearl is a small wheelchair-bound patient. Adjustment to the home was difficult for her and, like most of us, when life is difficult, she was negative. This attitude persisted for a long time. We tried a game. "On my next visit, tell me five good things that happened to you." It worked! Over a period of weeks, the frown left her face. Now Pearl has good things to say about her home.

Simone has been in the nursing home for a long time and is now quite feeble. His mind, always somewhat confused, is no longer able to direct his speech. Simone liked to relate fantasy tales of events in Burma where he was in military service. He would become quite dramatic and wave his arms in gestures suited to his story. In earlier years, his attendance at our nursing home mass was a Christmas event only. He would put on his Sunday coat and tie, and would genuflect reverently in the lobby where we were to have mass. He now attends every service, but omits the genuflection due to stiffness.

Edith is unable to talk. On one of my visits, I picked up an open scrap book from the floor next to her bed. The pages were crumpled and soiled from much use. My eyes rested on the open page, which showed a puppy dog cuddling a small kitten. Above the picture were hand printed words, "Too tired to walk, so I will carry you"—a good message for one bringing the Eucharist to weary Edith. In her confusion and discomfort, Edith always nods to the question, "Would you like to receive Holy Communion?" She receives a tiny piece because she is tube fed. Her eyes close and Edith is like the small kitten in the paws of the puppy. Jesus is her friend and consoler.

Rollin, now blind, had belonged to a well known band that played throughout the country. A beat-up picture above his bed shows him playing the saxophone. Today he sits in his wheel chair trying to tune a Mandolin an employee brought him. His frustrations were strongly verbal as he plucked away at the strings. One string off key caused a winced face and loud request, "Get me a screw driver or a monkey wrench." This man knows good music. Now, in his aging blindness, family and friends are gone. There is no one close to visit him.

Josie was a saintly quadriplegic who lived with her mother until her mother's death. Both were cared for by Alice, one of Josie's sisters, who fully dedicated herself to their care. Josie needed total help which included being fed. Her speech was not clear to me, but Alice always understood and shared Josie's humor and wisdom with me. Josie's eyes and smile glowed with love and delight for any visitor. Visitors always left with her special gift of self. Her Momma's loving eyes were always on Josie, who, when she was able, had helped her Momma on the ranch at one time. Momma had come from Austria, married and raised a big family through many hardships. Stories told to me by Alice and her sister, Edith, were unforgettable. They were tops among my dear friends.

Postscript: 2007 Momma died first and Josie several years later. Loving family members have beautiful memories of both.

~ ~ ~ ~ ~ ~ ~

MEET MORE OF MY FRIENDS

written for and printed in a Province newsletter

1988

During my parish ministry work at nursing homes in the 1980s, many of the elderly people I served became cherished friends. Some of them were especially memorable. Here are vignettes of some of them:

Cliff sleeps comfortably in his wheelchair, no longer able to give his favorite message, "I was an altar boy for fifteen years." Another new baseball cap on his aged head speaks of a caring family. Faith lives on in sleep!

Susan loves to chat! Holding a beat-up, hand-carved walking stick, she tells of her a happy days cooking for Sisters in Wisconsin. Susan never fails to mention the Holy Spirit and wonders if the world can be saved. Hope is alive!

Albert made sausages in his Chicago factory and he comes to life when this topic is mentioned. A stroke took his speech but his hands and a few crumpled words convey his interest. Thank God for Faith to fight!

Mary's fragile, arthritic condition accounts for constant pain. Yet, she always has a gentle smile and is eager to receive our Lord in the Eucharist. A sign of hope indeed!

Sophie is proud of her Polish heritage and the ability to fight for justice. Her sometimes humorous demands for proper care command respect and attention from the staff. Faith in action!

Nina is gentle and loving, and always expresses how good God is. One day she said, "My mother was killed in an accident last night, but she is with God now." Lifelong faith in peace!

Charles, at eighty-five, has just lost both legs above the knees. Poor circulation never erased his gentle courtesy. "The grace of God is in courtesy." – G.K.C.

Claire is forty and retarded. To each person who greets her, they receive a cheerful, "I like you!" God dwells in the simple!

Abelarbo never talks. He is from Cuba and no one knows his story. A sign of the cross brings a knowing smile from him. One time he agreed to be Zacchaeus as we read the Gospel at a service. Jesus surely has a permanent residence in his house!

Alice reads and talks about books. She has a Ph.D. and taught English for years. She never felt good about herself because of childhood scars. The Kingdom of Heaven is hers!

Gloria is one of the many aides and housekeepers who bring faithful, loving care and humor to the elderly. Not for $$$ does she work! Blessed are the generous!

These are but very brief glimpses into the lives of only a few of many valued friends. I am reminded of an African saying, "A library burns down every time an old person dies." Would that we could read these libraries better and change the world through their wisdom.

~ ~ ~ ~ ~ ~ ~

MUSINGS OF A MINISTER TO THE ELDERLY

Several years ago, when I was interviewed for a job as Minister to the Elderly, Father Bill informed me there were five nursing homes in the parish. My verbal reaction came quickly. "Forget it!" But Father Bill encouraged me to listen as he outlined the services needed in each home—an alternating of regular masses, sacrament of the sick, communion services, and special visits as needed. I agreed to give it a try. From day one, every visit has been a life-giving experience, a real blessing indeed.

The elderly teach me, by their quiet lives, the real meaning of love. Their example of faith, prayer, wisdom, goodness and humor are but a few of the wonderful gifts shared with me through example and communication.

My elderly friends are interesting and lovable. Each one is unique in personality and outlook. Their candor and humor often amaze me. Seeing Jesus in a bedridden patient, in one in severe arthritic pain, in a bewildered Alzheimer's sufferer or in a feisty gray-haired man or woman, is easier at times, I must admit, than always recognizing His presence in my own Sisters in Community. Such encounters are an ongoing challenge in my spiritual life.

In the aged, Christ's presence radiates from each countenance as long years of struggles and victories culminate in peace and calmness. Some faces, it is true, reveal traces of pain, loneliness, mystery. One need only listen and visit with a person to find an underlying resignation and serenity in most persons. Visiting and praying with my friends lightens their more serious memories. The elderly often wait for a listening ear.

Occasionally, there has been the experience of encountering spiritual immaturity or a lack of understanding of the real meaning of life. Rose is one such case.

Repeatedly she told me, "Oh, I'm so proud to be a Catholic." In the next breath she would bitterly criticize the nursing home or rail about a son who never came to see her. We talked and prayed about her hurts and anger but there was little or no change.

Finally, at a nurse's frustration with Rose's discontent, I resorted to a tough love approach and confronted her with the hypocrisy of pride in being a Catholic. Rose began to look at herself and now, in her mid-eighties, is trying to give and forgive in order to honestly be a good Catholic.

Maggie was difficult to love. She demanded complete attention every time I approached her. There was no consideration for others around her who also needed help. I would bristle with irritation. There was only one solution—love Maggie through prayer, patience, and common sense. She needed my attention no matter what. An effort was made to take time, approach her kindly, and listen. After many months, Maggie's face wore a smile instead of a frown. Her self-esteem was more apparent.

Mindfulness through prayer and quiet was the key to finding and loving Christ in Pearl. Needless to say, such experiences are a call to look within myself and practice what I preach.

Appreciation of the smallest kindness is a noticeable trait in my friends. A short visit, a handshake, a smile, a candy shared with attention to the person brings forth a smile of gratitude from a heart in touch with God.

I recall Peg, a nursing home resident who slipped an envelope into my hand after a communion service one day. A note on the envelope said, "Something for your coffee break." Inside was a coffee, a creamer and two cookies—a valued gift of love. This is a cherished memory that came from a grateful heart now stilled.

Celebration of the Eucharist in mass, or more simply in a communion service, is a high point in the week for many. Their eagerness to see the priest, to receive the Eucharist, and periodically the Sacrament of the Sick, is very meaningful. Hearing familiar hymns, reciting prayers of the mass or Hail Mary's, renews memories of the past and strengthens them on their journey homeward. Room visits to the elderly are a valued blessing for both of us.

My friends have learned to talk with God in their lonely hours instead of being disgruntled if a phone call or visit does not come their way. Their talking with God is rather a listening and a waiting for Him, while quietly reviewing memories of years long past. God is present to them in memories.

In talking about death with the aged, there is seldom any fear of it. Most often they look forward to leaving this world for a better life. Some long for God's coming. One man even had a bit of humor—"It sure beats this place; I'm ready to go right now."

Over the years, I have said goodbyes to many valued friends and watched them depart peacefully. Each passing is a reminder to face the reality of death in my own life and to live each moment in grateful awareness.

Truly my ministry with the elderly is a daily challenge to "—act justly, love tenderly, and walk humbly with my God." *—Micah*

~ ~ ~ ~ ~ ~ ~

MY TICKET TO AN ADVENTURE

July, 1990

A few weeks ago, I read in the Sunday paper about the summer ski train that was operating, for the first summer, as a Saturday outing to Winter Park. Sounded so good I posted the clipping to find a companion for such a day. The cost was forty-five dollars. I had that much in my envelope marked "Elderly," so I qualify for a treat, thinks I. Well, nobody signed up, so I decided to call for reservations and go it on my own. 'Twas a good idea because there was only one day left when I could get a reservation. Other dates were already filled.

The day arrived and Sr. Paula drove me to Union Station at six-forty-five A.M. so I could board the ten-car ski train at seven-fifteen A.M. A few backpackers and some Oldies were the first to get on the train. 'Twas great fun to watch the nearly one thousand people scurry to get on as I watched from my seat near the window. Armed with a cup of coffee and a thermal lunch box, I was on my way. Promptly at eight A.M. the train pulled out. We had a perfect map that pointed out important signs along the way. We went through twenty-three tunnels—some very short, others longer. The scenery was indescribable as we climbed to over nine thousand feet—mountains, canyons, swift creeks flowing over boulders and brush. My seat companion was a grandma who was with her family across the aisle. We talked a little. She had moved here from New York City. She had a Jesuit brother and a sister who joined the convent. She knew every curve the train made as she had taken Amtrak with her husband so many times. We were to arrive in Winter Park at ten-fifteen. The last lap was Moffett Tunnel—six-and-two-tenths miles, a ten to fifteen minute jaunt—and when we saw daylight, we were at Winter Park.

People, including mostly families with children, spilled out of the ten cars and made for the Park which was just on the other side of a board fence. Spread out was a village of shops. There were amusements of different kinds including a ski lift, alpine slide, miniature golf, etc. We did not go into the nearby town.

My ticket, which turned out to be forty dollars for seniors, included one of the above. I had no intention of going on the rides. Instead, I intended to read, reflect and watch people.

The more I watched the lifts and slide, the more curious I became. So I picked out a few gray heads to ask how they enjoyed it. The first man said, "I'm seventy-five and took my grandson. You'd enjoy it! Go to the information tent and get a free year-round ticket for all these events for people over seventy-five." After talking with an eighty-seven-year-old woman from Atlanta who had done them all, I went for the free ticket, then stood in line for the lift that would take me to the Alpine Slide.

The line was long. A twelve-year-old Greg marked my place while he slid along on the fence and I'd find a seat ahead. We both arrived for our turn and agreed to have the same swing seat. He fastened us in and away we went.

I had not one bit of panic as I had experienced on the Ferris wheel with Sr. Armella Weibel back in the summer of 1936 before we entered the convent. This ride was pure joy. Trees, sky, everything looked brighter. We could see hikers following paths below and bicycles on other paths.

At the top we got out and stood in line to come down on the three thousand foot slide. Greg quickly hoisted my plastic sled-like vehicle into one trough, then hoisted his into the other trough while I got my arthritic limbs into the sled. There was a handle in the middle that controlled the speed. Soon I saw Greg start off at high speed while I waited for others in front of me. We were spaced about fifteen feet apart on the run.

My start was modest speed but when I saw a child wanting to go fast as we went around the next curve, I speeded up and watched the signs carefully as we flew around the others.

Greg was at the bottom laughing. "And how'd you like it?" "Wonderful!" Actually there was inner praise to God for the new experience I never dreamed would happen. WOW!

Greg started on another lift after we exchange goodbyes. He's a bright lad who wants to be an architect. I told him to tell his parents how kind he was to this old nun. We are friends.

Walking in space, I headed for a bench in the shade to have some lunch. A gray head was glad to have someone to talk with. She had just had a bite at one of the expensive shops, so did not share my lunch. She was there with her daughter and husband and twin two-year-old daughters. They had come on the train also.

Now it was time to go on the really high lift near by that takes the skiers up. It is the highest lift in this country. The line for this was shorter and I shared a ride with two college brothers from Arkansas. They took their bikes which were hung on the back of seats, alternating with people seats. They were friendly and the lift was again very exhilarating though it did not go very fast. At the very top of Winter Park Mountain, we can see far and wide below and above in all directions. Awesome indeed!

This time two women invited me to ride down with them. One must have been a social worker who was treating a client to the ride. She knew of Marycrest and had sent someone there for help. Another good person.

I thought it best not to try any more rides since we were to start for the train about two P.M. It was to leave at two-thirty so I visited and just looked about. People watching is fun.

The trip home was another prayerful, joyful experience. To really experience God's beauty and the gifts around us is to be one with Him.

Sister Helen met me at the station and was amazed at the number of people pouring out of those ten cars. She listened and rejoiced with me over this overwhelming experience. What a wonderful day it was!

~ ~ ~ ~ ~ ~ ~

MYSTERIOUS SYMPHONY

November, 2006

One morning, after dressing and getting ready to go to morning prayer, I was treated to lovely, soft music. The source of it seemed to be in my room, but then I decided it was my neighbor's radio and left.

Later, when I returned to my room, the symphony was still there. I went next door, but found there was no radio music. So I carefully walked my room, with ears tilted to hear where the music was coming from—under the bed, maybe the closet?

The search led to the wastebasket. I reached down to find a singing birthday card that had sprung. It had entertained me all night but I couldn't hear it until my hearing aid was in place.

Thank heaven for symphonies!

~ ~ ~ ~ ~ ~ ~

NAME GAME

Beginning about 1999, I sometimes find enjoyment in penning complimentary mini-descriptions of the Sisters in my profession group, of my Community members, and of others. To begin, I write the letters spelling a person's name in vertical order. Then opposite each letter, I write two words that described that person as I know them. Occasionally I include a full name, but most often, I use just the first name. Also, the use of a dictionary can stimulate thoughts of words one might not normally recall.

Here I've included a partial list of the names I used for my own Name Game. As you read each one, try to visualize the person for whom it was written. Could be, some of you readers will recognize a description of yourself or of someone you know.

If you read far enough down my list, I believe you, too, will catch on to the thought process required to do this. I challenge you to play this Name Game by starting with your own name. Enjoy!

Mirthful Martha
Always amiable
Refreshingly real
Teasingly therapeutic
Humorous, happy
Ardent, avant-garde

Valiant Vaughn
Astute, alert
Understanding, untiring
Godly giver
Hopeful, helpful
Never negligent

Loving listener
Intense, interesting
Zealous, zestful

Dear, daring Debbie
Endless endurance
Big hearted, brave
Balanced behavior
Indispensable indeed
Enables, enlivens

Sincere, sociable
Always affable
Radiates rainbows
Alive, astute
Happy, human

Polite, prayerful
Apt, attentive
Unobtrusive, unassuming
Lovely Latino
Approachable, amiable

Christ centered
Affable, adaptable
Refined, responsible
Mature, mannerly
Excellent example
Noble, notable

Likable, literate
Open, optimistic
Insightful, intelligent
Successful, social

Happy, humorous
Enlivens, enables
Never naughty
Responsible, receptive
Intense, interested
Earnest, effective
Tactful, thoughtful
Tolerant, thankful
Apt, astute

Sunny, serene
Earnest, educable
Normal, yet note-worthy

Cordial, creative
Optimistic, outgoing
Responsible, resourceful
Respectful, reliable
Intelligent, interesting
Never naughty, no-nonsense
Enables, efficient

Kindly
Always affable
Reverent, reliable
Effective educator
Nurturing, receptive

Mature, mannerly
Astute, ardent
Courageous Christian
Responsible, resourceful
Indomitable, intense
Notable, no-nonsense
Apt, adaptable

Listens, laughs
Effective, educator
Obliging, outgoing
Never neglectful
Always approachable

Human, (w)holesome
Endless endurance
Laughing, likeable
Enlivening, enriching
Nature loving

Keen, kind
Always alert
Tolerant, tough
Helpful, humorous
You're youthful

Hopeful, helpful
Effective, empathetic
Listens, loves
Excellent endurance
Never noisy
Avid artist

Responsible, respectful
Understanding, untiring
Tolerant, thoughtful
Human, happy

Always accountable
Never negligent
Tenacious, tranquil
Observant, outgoing
Noble, noteworthy
Indifferent, illuminative
Always affable

Experienced, efficient
Usually understanding
Shock proof
Thoughtful, tough
Apt, approachable
Catholic to the core
Initiative, inventive
Active, accountable

Excellent educator
Long suffering, literate
Exhibits endurance
Never neglectful
Illumines individuals
Upright, uplifting
Spiritually solicitous

Self-confident, sincere
Hopeful, humorous
Efficient educator
Intense, interesting
Likeable, life-giving
Adaptive, approachable

Likable, life-giving
Efficient, elevating
Able, accountable
Nobody's nonsense
Daring, debonair
Righteously religious
Always adaptive

Chardin's child
Enlightened, efficient
Christian to the core
Intense, impartial
Life-giving, lenient
Interesting
Alive, alert

God's gift to a Province
Light, laughing
Outward to others
Relaxed, reasonable
Invincible, inviolate
Always Alert

~ ~ ~ ~ ~ ~ ~

NEWNESS OF SPRING

The newness of spring is evident in Helen's back yard. As we exit her back door, I see tulips peeping through the ground. We look at old arthritic fruit trees, a twisted apple tree, a cherry tree that looks more promising and, in a corner, an aging plum tree with many branches with green leaves emerging. Bird feeders extend from two of the trees and a small birdhouse rests in another. Near the backdoor is a low, homemade bird feeder that is laden with goodies for Helen's feathered friends.

"That will go soon," she says. "It's spring. The birds can soon find their own food."

Walking down the cement walk to the back of the garden, one spies a small shed for tools. It has served well over the years, as its well weathered board siding shows. A rusty padlock holds a creaky door in place to protect Helen's garden tools. To one side of the shed, we examine more green shoots peeping through the winter's collection of brown leaves and twigs. Some plants appear to be lilies of the valley. Others have small purple blossoms. Each of us ponders the beauty and sacredness of life quietly.

Hanging above this small corner plot is a grape arbor with vines already climbing along the aging boards. At this point, Helen tells about the grape jelly and juice she canned last fall and that she is looking forward to a good yield again this year.

As we quietly return to the house, our senses are experiencing full enjoyment of the newness of spring. Once inside, I am asked to be seated while Helen pours a glass of her home canned grape juice. We enjoy this treat and each other's company, as we share an awareness of God's gifts to us.

~ ~ ~ ~ ~ ~ ~

NURSING HOMES

Nursing homes are among my favorite places. For over twenty years, my ministry has been to the elderly residents in five nursing homes—Sheridan Care Center, Wheatridge Manor, Cedar Health Care Center, Glen Ayr Nursing Home and Cambridge Care Center.

These homes are located within the boundaries of St. Mary Magdalen Parish, thus the parish is responsible for the spiritual care of Catholics in the above facilities. At one time there was a cancer hospital and a home for retarded which were also on the parish list. Both of these facilities are now closed.

In the beginning, when I was asked to do this work, it appeared to be too much. However, I gave it a try and found that I had a gift for remembering names and for caring about each resident. It was not long before I had some one-hundred-sixty dear friends in the five homes. Of course they were in various stages of mental and physical conditions. What that was, made no difference. It was a call to give concerned care and love as each one needed. For one, it could be gentle gossip; another, special prayer; for the down-in-spirit, a joke. The hard of hearing and bed patients needed touch, just as normal patients, but more so. The blind like to hear about happenings and a description of the flower that might be nearby.

For those who could attend our bi-weekly services, the services had special meaning. It is like attending a service in church. One attends to listen to the word and to join others in prayer, as they prepare to receive our Lord in Holy Communion. All residents, in every home and in every service, I found, in general, to be very attentive even though many could not hear. I recall one lady years ago who was blind. I watched her as the priest offered mass. At the consecration, she reverently struck her breast as the Bread and Wine were offered. What faith one sees in the in elderly!

Of course, an occasional Alzheimer patient might disrupt the service by wanting out, or mumbling, or yelling. Such disruptions were brief and seldom in number.

After Communion Service, occasionally, I'd try to tell an appropriate joke they could get. Usually a small number would responded with broad smiles and an open laugh. Satisfaction indeed.

As I look back, it is with gratitude for the hundreds, possibly thousands, of friends I've made over a period of twenty-plus years. Volunteer visits still keep me in touch with the most wise and beautiful people in the world.

~ ~ ~ ~ ~ ~ ~

OLD STORY – NEW ENDING

A prayerful distraction during a morning meditation
based on *The Little Red Hen* story
from the 1920s Winston Reader
September, 2006

The little red hen found some wheat. She called the cat. She called the goose. She called the pig.

"Who will help me plant the wheat?"

"Not I," said the cat.

"Not I," said the goose.

"Not I," said the pig.

"Then I will plant the wheat," she said.

The wheat grew ripe and the little red said, "Who will help me harvest the wheat?"

"Not I," said that cat.

"Not I," said the goose.

"Not I," said the pig.

"Then I will harvest the wheat," she said.

"Who will help me make the flour?" the little red hen asked.

"Not I," said the cat.

"Not I," said the goose.

"Not I," said the pig.

"Then I will make the flour," she said.

"Who will help me make the bread?" the little red hen asked.

"Not I," said that cat.

"Not I," said the goose.

"Not I," said the pig.

"Then I will bake the bread," she said.

"Who will help me eat the bread?"

"I will," said the cat.

"I will," said the goose.

"I will," said the pig.

The little red hen invited them to sit down and enjoy the bread. They did so and left with remorse and repentance, gratitude and love in their hearts. A community was reborn with the Little Red Christ as its head.

~ ~ ~ ~ ~ ~ ~

ONE FOR THE MONEY

written in a time of temporary exasperation
1980s

"One for the money,
Two for the show,
Three to get ready and
Four to go!"

That old rhyme from a kids game in days of yore comes to mind occasionally at meal time. In the convent, it may or may not be different from other orders, groups or organizations who dine together. One thing for certain we all have in common—the instinct of self-preservation. At meal time it comes to life and cries, "Eat!" As we proceed to the dining room in small groups after prayer together, or if we amble in one by one, there is small talk among the nuns. But once in the dining room, it appears that environment has much to do with appetite.

My interesting observation at this time I call the Security Game. We sit down on or stand behind the chair of our choice. For some, this is a comfortable, secure selection, depending on companions who feel likewise. To ensure a mealtime lease on this comfortable environment, the applicant for the cozy place grabs a cup, glass, napkin, salt, pepper, sugar shaker, anything within reach—I've never seen a comb or shoe—to use as a marker. The renter plops down the object and reservation is complete. Only the foolhardy would remove the reserved ticket. I think this has happened by mistake at times, depending on the position of the reserved object. If it is not visibly situated right in the middle of a selected space, someone else seeking a space is apt to sit down to enjoy her meal. This could cause minor insecurity for the person who lost her place. Alas! I have never witnessed any major problems over this error, unless it would be the embarrassment of the person who discovered she was in a chosen spot.

After the security transaction, it is safe to get in the chow line. Then the emphasis is on food. Because we have cafeteria service, we try to keep moving as we pickup our meal. For those with the reserved tickets, I think the food must taste better and the meal, perhaps, is more enjoyable. For those who choose not to lease a spot, there is no problem, unless it's a feeling of being left out.

In our dining room there are plenty of tables. If there are no free spaces, one can join our elderly ladies, the men, or even choose a whole table to herself, where sometimes latecomers will join. One thing is certain, there is always plenty of food. God always provides even to those who choose not to secure a reservation. How grateful we can be!

~ ~ ~ ~ ~ ~ ~

POINSETTIAS

Christmas would not be the same if we were to be without poinsettias. They are an essential part of this great feast. Their beautiful red petals emphasize the symbol of love, the true meaning of Christmas.

At this festive season the flower shops and other stores are full of this red beauty. Drivers can be seen in many places delivering this love gift to family and friends who happily receive them.

This past Christmas, I was with Mary, an eighty-five-year-old widow. Two days before Christmas the doorbell rang. A delivery man had a box of beautiful poinsettias and handed me one for Mary. She was delighted and quickly looked at the tag. "From Connie," she remarked and added, "She always does the nicest things. When she makes lasagna or any special dish, she always shares it with three of us who are her neighbors."

The poinsettia was a six-inch pot size with bold, bright petals and leaves. Sitting in the middle of Mary's small, round kitchen/dining room table, it brightened the whole apartment. The pretty gold ribbon on the pot and a small label revealed it was from the town's lovely flower and gift shop. What joy Connie gave to her friends who would not, otherwise, have received a poinsettia.

Seeing Mary's joy at her lovely gift, I was reminded of another Christmas season some years ago. I visited Violet, a resident of a nearby housing project. On her front door was tacked an ad from a Target store sale flyer. It pictured a large Christmas tree with poinsettias arranged at the bottom. Poor as the ornament was, there was beauty in the picture. Inside Violet's apartment there was warmth, love and joy as her lonely door-picture exemplified.

Churches and chapels are filled with poinsettias at Christmas time. What uplifting joy they bring to the congregation. This year when I attended Mass with Mary at her church, I counted thirty-six potted poinsettias in front of the altar, put there by individual families and members of the church. There were also poinsettias at other places in the church giving glory to God.

Reflecting on the joy given to Mary and others, I resolve to write to the pastor, a good, kind, spiritual man, to make this suggestion—next year when planning church decorations, perhaps it could be suggested that families seek out a person or family who never received a poinsettia and give them one. It would still be possible to have the lovely flowers in church but fewer in number.

Because churches usually are filled only on Sundays and Feast days, the flowers in many churches are alone all week. I'd like to think our Lord would encourage my idea of bringing the joy of poinsettias to others.

Postscript: A later discussion on this topic led to the decision, "Let people make their choice."

~ ~ ~ ~ ~ ~ ~

QUILTING

1990s

Sister Elizabeth just asked me if I can help with a project for the food-clothing bank. It was, she explained, tying quilts to be given to the needy. We agreed to find volunteers and, at a later date, we could arrange a quilting party.

For many years, Margaret F. has been making quilts to be given to the needy through the food-and-clothing bank. As I recall, this Good Samaritan was a retired schoolteacher. Fabric shop managers save remnants of colorful materials that she collects and sews into attractively arranged quilt covers. No two are alike. These covers are sewed over a flannel lining with warm filling in between.

Margaret, I am told, makes a quilt in two days. In the winter time she works regularly so there will be plenty of quilts available for giveaway. At this time, about two dozen quilts are waiting to be tied.

My plan is to call for volunteers and arrange a day with Sister Liz for a quilting party. It can be a fun afternoon with chitchat and possibly a sharing of some memories from older folks who may still recall the real quilting parties of early days.

The party will be an opportunity for self giving as we are reminded of its real purpose—to provide warmth of body and love of heart to any and all who are recipients of Margaret's love gift, quilts.

Postscript: 2007 The quilting party was truly a fun time and a huge stack of quilts got tied.

Later on, I also joined a quilting group that met at Highland Senior Center on Monday mornings. Some cut, others arranged pieces, two sewed on the machine, and others tied quilts. It was a fun morning as we shared jokes and chatter as well. At Christmas time we had a nice party to celebrate our accomplishments.

~ ~ ~ ~ ~ ~ ~

RAPHAEL

Raphael is a six-year-old boy who has been staying at Marycrest with his mother while she works and looks for a house.

Raphael is a very bright, happy boy who has lots of energy. He can scoot across the floor in seconds and arrive at the other of the room in no time. He can ask more questions in a short time than any adult I know.

One evening Raphael taught me to play Uno, a very simple card game. Guess who won most often? Yes, Raphael. After several games, he appeared bored and chose to watch a video that had been set up for him.

Raphael is always courteous, obedient to his mother and never takes a piece of candy or assumes other privileges without first asking.

Watching us play Scrabble one evening, he spelled the word s-c-r-a-b-b-l-e by looking at it backwards on the box lid. Later I put my hand over the word and he spelled it perfectly.

He and his mother are great friends. We will miss them when they leave.

~ ~ ~ ~ ~ ~ ~

RED

I saw **red**! We are in the **red**! Go Big **Red**!

These are a few of the slogans we use to express surprise, something out of the ordinary. It's a color that speaks its own name; a color that awakens, cheers, surprises!

Red! I've been told it can make a bull angry. How well I recall my little sister and me hanging onto a wire fence while waving a big red kerchief at a bull on the other side. We were ready to run if the bull charged. Alas! It did nothing to disturb him. We wondered about that common belief.

Red brings people to life when it is worn in dress. Depending on personalities, it fits some better than others. Only in my old age do I sometimes wear red. My friends in the nursing homes like it, but it took many years for me to change from black, to navy or brown, to the bright red.

Yes, **red** is a color that's alive and well. I like **red**.

~ ~ ~ ~ ~ ~ ~

REFLECTIONS ON MATURITY

"Oh she's just immature." "It takes longer for some people to grow up." "She's number so-and-so on the Enneagram."

All of these, and more of such worn-thin phrases, heard in earlier years, ring in my ears. Memories return of struggling, strangling situations that wrenched the heart and pricked the head in valiant efforts to grow up. Other memories are of countless failures to be and do and say the right thing at the right time. Such fruitless efforts they were, so it seems, to be one of the bunch.

Occasional successes brought exhilaration and spared a caustic glance or word from the mighty and mature who knew victory.

Why such wasted fears and futile efforts to conquer human weakness—to appear okay?

'Twould be nice to be like others who seemed to have it made. In aging years, life goes on, as God's grace still filters faithfully and forcefully to insulate the cracks and crevices of my being.

Joy! God accepts and loves me the way I am. Lord, thank you for delivering me from what people think!

~ ~ ~ ~ ~ ~ ~

RETREAT

written at the beginning and at the end of a five-day retreat
1990s

Day 1—As I ponder plans for a few desert days, I find myself gazing on a many-branched dead tree. It's a tall tree with many dangling, crooked limbs and some broken by the weight of snow. I wonder why the owner has not cut it down? Could it be that the job is too costly? Perhaps they are hoping to coax some life from it in its apparent state of dying.

The tree speaks of life. We too have broken, crooked limbs, some twisted under the burden of daily living. One thing is certain—the total outline of the tree is strong and beautiful.

Did not Jesus say, "I am the vine, you are the branches?" As I ponder this thought, the branches on one side of the tree come to life—yes, there are tiny green leaves gathering—enough to say, "I am alive and struggling."

Then, as I examine the tree for more life, it is plain to see that the top branches are greening with ever so tiny leaves. The sun's rays touched them first and they are responding. So, too, we green and grow when we can bask in God's love.

Day 5—It's amazing how the tree has burst forth in green—all of it—the crooked, dangling limbs are hidden under the healthy branches. The tree is a pleasing whole.

So, too, we—the scars of life can be hidden under the mantle of God's Mercy. Baptismal graces can bloom and blossom only if we let God love us and shower us with His mercy.

Lord, for this grace, I ask, "—to know You, to love You, to follow You each day, for the rest of my life." Only in this way can I be like the green, growing tree, giving shade and protection to others along the way.

~ ~ ~ ~ ~ ~ ~

"SHAKE AWAKE"

early 1990s

Recently I became a very satisfied owner of a Shake Awake clock; that is, after I learned the many little tricks it took to make the clock work. Until then, I cussed technology more than once when it failed to work because of a failed procedure to press the right button.

The clock was invented for the hard of hearing who fail to hear an ordinary alarm clock, even a Big Ben. The small black box has a vibrator that one sets according to instructions. At the right time, I hear (feel) the rumbling and I'm awake. No more excuse for being late for Community morning prayer.

This magic box was found after a search for some device that would get me up on time. A flashing light was what I had in mind. Then I learned, through a hearing agency, of a store in Englewood that carried a vibrator clock. A call was made and a cheerful voice said they would be sending me a catalog in the mail on that day.

Pronto! It arrived the next day. A device was found that cost seventy-some dollars. With delivery, the charge would be eighty-two dollars and some cents. It was agreed that the instrument would benefit me and the community so a check was sent off immediately. The miracle machine was to arrive in a few days.

While waiting for its arrival, a small ad was placed on my desk one day. Very briefly, it told of a Shake Awake clock that cost twenty-four dollars. It could be obtained through an eight-hundred number. The ad was in an AARP magazine so I knew it was reliable.

The time for arrival of the vibrator clock was now over a week. A call was made to see if it was on its way. The billing department said no check had arrived so the order was canceled. A few days later the check was returned.

During this time, I am calling the eight-hundred number whenever there was a free moment—but always a busy signal or gap for a recording. After several frustrating days of such efforts, I found the *Modern Maturity* magazine in which the ad was found. Page after page I looked for a number but that would put me in touch with their offices. About ready to give up, I landed an insurance ad in the magazine that had an eight-hundred number. A prompt call received a prompt answer. A kindly man gave me another number to call after I explained my need. This call was answered by another kind, male voice who knew of the ad. He said, "Keep calling." When I told him of my efforts of many days, he put me on hold, then returned and said, "They are answering now." I figured they were responding to his area and not mine, so I begged him to put my order through for me. Again he listened and put me on hold. In seconds, a female voice said, "Shake Awake." I could have hugged her if I had been close enough.

The kindly lady could not send and bill me for this life-saver, but she'd send a catalog. "Thank you, thank you," and we parted voices.

Three days from New Jersey and the catalog was in my mailbox. Sue agreed to send off the order the same day with the check for twenty-four dollars plus the four dollars handling charges. No time was lost.

In a week or so the package arrived, to the joy of all who were anticipating, along with me, the arrival of Shake Awake. It took three or four helpers to read the instructions and then no response from the box the next morning. I was still late. We had failed to set it correctly.

It was placed in my mailbox until clock doctors could observe and advise. Promptly at six P.M. Kathy called me and said, "Your clock is vibrating." Sure enough, Shake Awake could be heard (felt) in the hallway. What rejoicing! Unless I fail to set it for A.M. instead of P.M., the magic box is doing its job.

Instead of going on the road to advertise, the good news of my find is passed on by written and spoken word. One hundred cheers for Shake Awake!

~ ~ ~ ~ ~ ~ ~

SURPRISES

1980s

One bright spring day—Easter Monday to be exact—was a day of unexpected surprises. My goal was to bring joy to a blind friend,

Philippine, by surprising her with an Easter basket.

As I was cruising on an unfamiliar street, a glance in the rear view mirror revealed a policeman on a motorcycle. No lights were flashing but a gentle siren signaled me to pull over.

When policeman in helmet approached me, I said, "Are you checking drivers' licenses today?"

With a stern expression he said, "Give me your drivers license."

As he was examining it I thought, "You're safe. The license is good for eight months." Then my friend in helmet said, "Lady, you were going thirty-seven miles an hour in a twenty-five mile an hour zone." Next he presented me with a ticket and said, "You may pay the fine or go to court."

Heavens, who ever heard of going to court over a speeding ticket? With a polite, "Thank you, sir," I place the ticket in my pocket for later a surprise.

With senses sharpened by the unexpected reminder, the signs along the road read, "twenty-five mph, twenty-five mph, twenty-five mph." How could I have been so blind?

After my visit with Philippine, all unpleasant thoughts were erased and I felt renewed by her inner vision.

Back home the yellow slip was removed from my pocket. The fine print in small boxes, carefully read, brought the next surprise, a forty-seven dollar fine. "Outrageous!" was my first reaction. "Just think," I said to myself, "a forty-seven dollar fine for my first offense!" A friend checked the document and found it to be no mistake.

At this point, the words of my helmeted friend resounded loudly, "You must pay the fine or go to court." Quick reference to the fine print read, "You may enter a plea of guilty or nolo contendere."

After translating the Latin and turning down advice of friends, to just pay the fine because it is cheaper, I stubbornly opted for court.

It took several calls and as many computer mistakes before the correct date was given, September twenty-eighth, eight a.m. The lady assured me a written notice would be in the mail. To make sure I'd have it on the calendar I promptly circled August twenty-eight, eight

A.M.—**COURT**—on two calendars. I was now free to forget the matter for the next five months.

On the eve of my court appearance, I made a list of reasons for the judge that read, "I am guilty of speeding but it is my first offense—I believe forty-seven dollars is too much to pay—It was a new area of driving for me and I was thinking thirty-five instead of twenty-five—I am a senior citizen and would like to keep my record clean." I then remembered a caption I read earlier in the day that now loomed before me. "Excuses are lies." The list was promptly terminated and went to bed.

Arising early, I gave myself plenty of time to drive downtown. There I found a parking space near the Cathedral. Through its big doors, I entered and paused long enough to say, "Lord, I'm not really here for a visit. I came for a free parking space. I am on my way to the courtroom."

I was forty-five minutes early and the second person in line. We scanned the long list of names of those to appear that day and mine was not among them. "Oh, I got lost in the computer," was my first thought. When the clerk appeared, I informed him of the deletion. Very patiently he said, "Come with me." One flip of a computer brought forth my Pentagon Pedigree. My friend then went to a large cupboard and brought forth one box, among many rows of boxes that contain numerous yellow slips, and, as fast as the computer produced, so his fingers located the evidence.

"It's what I thought. Your court date is **September** twenty-eighth, not August twenty-eighth," he said. I thanked him for his kind patience and left. Instead of punishing myself for error, I heeded the voice within that said, "Don't be upset. Take it in good humor." The clerk had just given me a fine example of that.

As I proceeded down the hallways, I noticed smiling faces and friendly chatter among the many people on their way to work. Once upstairs I glanced toward the end of the corridor and was surprised by a huge clown sculpture. The figure with legs in the air was resting on the palm of his right hand.

As I approached the sculpture, it surprisingly turned out to be an optical illusion. Painted on the wall was a black figure of a man doing a cartwheel. His left hand, in mid air, held a cigar. The message is clear! Don't take life too seriously! Take time to flip a cartwheel occasionally!

My way back to the car was full of other small surprises—friendly people, curious tourists, even a puppy dog.

Now as I await the final court day, I'm hoping the verdict will be a pleasant surprise instead of the, "I told you it would be cheaper to pay the fine."

Postscript: The arraignment process on September twenty-eighth was an excellent educational event. Being a senior and having a clean record earned for me a reduction in fine, a pleasant surprise at the end of a very long learning experience. I paid eighteen dollars, instead of forty-seven, with a smile of relief.

~ ~ ~ ~ ~ ~ ~

SYMBOLS OF HOPE

These ideas could be ways of bringing hope to others.

A **Hope Candle** symbolizing the Light of Christ, could be a symbol of hope for self and others, especially for anyone in need—the mentally ill, the despairing, the despondent persons who may be tempted to take their lives.

A **Hope Box** could be made from any kind of box. Cover it with pretty paper and put in it slips of paper on which you've written hope-thoughts and inspirations, such as a loving note received or sent, a picture or positive newspaper clipping. This is appropriate for both children and adults.

A **Scrapbook** of hope-and-joy pictures could be made by anyone who wants to give others a lift—the home bound, nursing home residents, a bored or hard working person. Anyone could benefit from good pictures or a collection of cartoons and funny jokes. Perhaps, make one to give yourself a lift.

~ ~ ~ ~ ~ ~ ~

THE THREE R's

June, early 1990s

Each summer I spend a few days in the mountains to brush up on these three R's—Rest, Respite, Renewal. These relaxing days among nature fulfill their purpose well. On my daily circle walk, there are interesting things to be seen. These are a few reflections that come easily.

Looking to the top, Long's Peak and surrounding mountains are partly covered with snow. I recall the Psalm, "I look to the mountains whence comes my help."

Looking below Long's Peak, the broad expanse of brown, dying pine is a shock indeed. In just a year's time this huge area has been struck by a blight and it is spreading rapidly. Even small pines are tinged with brown. It is a sad picture, but a good reminder of life and death.

Meditation on life and death comes easily as one surveys such a scene. Lord, make us mindful of our environment and do something to save it. Help us to get our own house in order before death calls.

As I continue on my circle walk, there are several patches of columbine plus a few standing alone, all to brighten the day. There is a strong urge to pick just one for our Communion altar, but state law comes to mind—also a reminder to resist temptation. Lord, you help us in so many ways!

Quiet cabin time encourages prayerful reflections and the

opportunity to put them into writing.

Yes, this time gives me Rest, Respite and Renewal!

~ ~ ~ ~ ~ ~ ~

TIME IS A PRECIOUS GIFT

February 26, 1985

Time is a precious gift. Do I value it as such? Precious gifts are handled with care and enjoyment. How is my handling of time? Sometimes, I let myself rush to get things done instead of planning well to get the most out of each hour, each moment.

There are miracles in each moment if I but see them—just being alive, being able to breathe, see, hear, think, enjoy the multitude of things provided by people and nature.

Time calls for decisions like the decision to write about time. As I write, people are moving about. One is going to work with people who need her time in love and care. Another is in a hurry to get somewhere. Hopefully there is a goal. One has returned from a trip and relates how her time was spent on the weekend. Others are enjoying a game of Casino.

Cards are a relaxing way to spend recreation time. I think of myself. My preference is scrabble. Sometimes we dally too long in searching for the right word, but that is not wasted time.

This evening I notice it is still quite light after dinner. The days are getting longer and we have the blessing of more daylight time. As I look back over this day there is a certain satisfaction that my time was fairly well spent. I can always do better. Tomorrow the sun will rise a little earlier than in bleak January. Hopefully, the day will be well planned and carried out so that each moment will have a purpose. If there are successes or failures, I will have tried to use my time well. Then there will be something in the Merit Bag for eternity.

Postscript: The above is a third try at writing on this subject. The others were meditative and personal, perhaps better. When I submitted this to the writing instructor for comments, this is what she wrote: "Although I do agree this could be more personal and less professional, nevertheless, it reveals a lot and gives a sense of person."

~ ~ ~ ~ ~ ~ ~

TRUFFLES

1990s

One of my hobbies is to try out a recipe, the result of which can be enjoyment or disaster.

Recently in the food section of the *Denver Post* were recipes for Valentine's Day Specialties. Among them was one for truffles. The word for me meant some kind of mysterious chocolate concoction. Now was my chance to really find out. The ingredients needed were semi-sweet or unsweetened chocolate, heavy cream and cocoa.

Shopping for the chocolate and cocoa was easy. But when I got to the dairy products display, no heavy cream. Thinking back to the milk and cream we had on the farm, I chose whipping cream.

Once home, I scalded one cup of the cream as directed. Into this I put the eight ounces of small pieces of the unsweetened chocolate, stirred it until it was smooth, and placed it in the fridge for four hours.

After removing it, I tasted the dark mixture. Ugh, it was bitter! Again, I looked at the recipe. No, there was no sugar called for. Truffles or not, they had to be sweet! So into the mixture I put powdered sugar, enough at least to resemble sweetness.

The next step called for was to spoon the mixture into small balls and roll it in cocoa. Again no sugar. My instinct knew better and powdered sugar with ground hazelnuts were added to the cocoa.

Now came the fun. Each small ball was made, rolled in the mixture and put aside to rest in a tin box in the refrigerator. The recipe said they would keep up to two weeks.

Samples were tasted. "Chocolatey." "Very Chocolatey." Other similar comments were made. No one asked for seconds.

Before the tin box could be passed around again, Valentine's Day arrived, as did a surprise box of real truffles! Needless to say, the real box of truffles was eagerly enjoyed, while the tin box timidly waits for the moment to give satisfaction, enjoyment or disappointment to someone craving chocolate.

The mysterious puzzle about no sugar in the recipe was explained by Sr. Helen who told us the history of truffles. They originated in England and were never meant to be sweet. The English enjoyed such chocolate with their tea. And so the recipe made the rounds in our world. Americans, I believe, added sugar.

This truffle experiment was an educational experience in the World of Chocolate. Bring on sweet truffles!

~ ~ ~ ~ ~ ~ ~

VALENTINE MEMORIES

1980s - Rev 1991, 2006

From the day after Christmas until February fourteenth, we are reminded that Valentine's Day is on its way. One can expect to see the various window displays and newspaper ads featuring love gifts ranging from Godiva chocolates and expensive roses to tiny teddy bears wearing hearts, and of course, valentines of every size and shape. A prospective buyer reflects on the symbol of the gift and decides to purchase it regardless of the price.

In reflecting on changes that have taken place, my memory evokes and savors valentine pictures of rural school days as one after another appears on my memory screen.

Valentines Day was an event to look forward to in our District #227 rural school in Nebraska. The bleak days in January and February in the 1920s and 1930s were brightened in anticipation of this day.

Weeks before February fourteenth, we would collect catalog pictures and scraps of paper. The school would provide some. Oh, the fun of that Friday afternoon before the big day—cutting and pasting valentines, and decorating ourselves as well, with flour and water paste.

If we were lucky enough to get scraps of paper doilies, the catalog pictures would be duly enhanced. Because Sears Roebuck and Montgomery Ward catalogs were almost the sole sources of pictures, we girls would cut out a prettily dressed girl or a stylish woman to adorn a red heart. Boys, to be silly, would cut out a pair of overalls or a piece of farm machinery and later send the funny valentine to a girlfriend.

The teachers usually prepared the big valentine box covered with red crepe paper, with a slit in the top. This would appear a few days ahead of time to receive the precious creations. Those who were lucky enough to send store-bought valentines were the envy of those who could not. These penny varieties had sentimental as well as humorous versus like, "Would you be mine?," "Valentine you're neat," "Roses are red—," and many more.

As the big day drew closer children could be seen putting their messages into the box as watchful eyes detected homemade or bought variety. For one observer there might be a secret hope that one would not be left out. For another, there would be the aspiration to win the un-sponsored popularity contest by receiving the most valentines. Hope was high until the afternoon of the fourteenth when the last hour of the school day was given to valentine exchange. Sometimes the teacher or a child would bring cookies with red sugar on top as a special treat.

Two children were selected to distribute the valentines as smiles and giggles followed. In a group of fifteen to twenty children, grades first through eighth, there was no doubt hidden disappointments also followed when a favorite friend or a secret lover failed to send a valentine or the right message. After the box was emptied the same questions buzzed from child to child, "How many 'didja' get?" "Who gave you that one?"

I recall one valentine with a picture of ladies slippers adorning the front. Inside the folded heart it said, "to Thecla from Walt." I was to deliver it later to my older sister at home. Of course, she laughed.

And there is another Valentines Day I recall pleasantly. It was the day I received my first valentine in the mail, at age nine or ten. It had been delivered to our mailbox on the road a half-mile away by the rural mail carrier. I can still see my former teacher's handwriting on the envelope with a two-cent stamp in the corner. Quickly I tore open the envelope. Out came a pretty valentine that unfolded to reveal a gorgeous red accordion-pleated heart on the front. Not only that, but the valentine could stand on its own for everyone to see. Above the big ruffled heart was a pretty girl and words like, "I love you." What ever the message, my interpretation was just that! On the back was my favorite teacher's writing. "To Catherine from Isabelle." So loudly did it speak of love and care, that, to this day, the memory of my first 'mail' valentine from a former teacher warms my heart.

Again this year, I shall buy a pretty valentine for Isabelle Koenig Thoendal who now resides in a nursing home. As it travels the skies, it will bear years of love and happy memories of my surprise 'mail' valentine. Joining people everywhere who send messages of love, my hearts will be delivered to nursing home residents and homebound elderly as we recall pleasant childhood memories of Valentine's Day.

As this story is being finished, a news item tells of Operation Valentine—a project of love and hope to send 400,000 valentines to our troops in the Gulf. Love is alive and growing!

Postscript: 2005 Throughout my own years of teaching elementary grades, Valentine's Day was an enjoyable one for both teacher and students. Later on, in nursing home ministry, it was great fun to make valentines for patients. We'd give parties each year on February fourteenth for the active elderly, a number of whom had attended rural school and who had their own valentine memories.

Now, at eighty-seven, I am in a nursing home myself but still able to make valentines. Now if I can just find the right catalogs?

~ ~ ~ ~ ~ ~ ~

WASTEBASKET

This important item may be a humble receptacle for trash, but it's mighty important for human beings everywhere.

Whether it be outdoors or inside a building, the wastebasket is an invitation for people to toss their discards. Its wide mouth is ever open to receive and never rejects a piece of trash. The container helps us human beings to keep our property looking respectable. Yes, there are always the slobs who are too lazy to dispose of garbage in the right way, even if the wastebasket reached out a hand to receive the trash.

Wastebaskets come in all sizes, all shapes. Some are of plastic, others are of metal. There are some made of straw while still others are made of heavy cardboard or other materials. They can be attractive and conceal the messy stuff that is tossed inside. Indeed wastebaskets are necessary and helpful. They fulfill an important need in this world of ours. Three cheers for wastebaskets!

~ ~ ~ ~ ~ ~ ~

WHY AM I HERE?

2005

We who are passing through this world must stop at times to think and ponder, "Why am I here?" The old catechism's answer to, "Why did God make you?" was "—to know Him, to love Him, to serve Him, and to be happy with Him for ever." Looking back, I, memorized this, but its meaning did not sink in. Sin, punishment, hell and damnation, did sink in—much too far! We were intent on saving our souls. For me, this fear had to be dug out by experiencing real love and justice, by learning of God's love through example and teaching. God, you saved me!

Yes, learning to know that God loves me took many years, with help from others, but it did grow. Today, at eighty-six, I am at peace in God's love, and that peace has brought about a good relationship with myself and others. Now I know what compassion is and share it, as I try to share respect and understanding as well. These gifts enable me to see the good in others. I know that differences accepted can make for greater togetherness and great mindfulness necessary for Community.

We can make this world a place where love is the center of our lives. Sharing it with joyful hope becomes contagious, and reaches far beyond our former puny selves. Even nature is included in our relationship as it calls us to appreciate beauty and motivates us to a higher quality of life. To live simply and honestly in our loving communities, while reaching out to help others, will make this world a place of kindness and peace.

~ ~ ~ ~ ~ ~ ~

As my first book, God's Brat, goes to press, I still write!

Epilogue

If you've come this far, Congratulations on your interest and perseverance!

We want you to know that nearly every time we met over the many steps in compiling this book together, Murt and I prayed for God's guidance and blessing on all who would read it. You will continue to be remembered in our prayers.

Now, if you have not already done so, please start writing down your own memoirs. You will find it to be fun and rewarding.

God bless!!

—Sr. Kathryn
January 30, 2007

At prayer, in thankfulness and gratitude

About the Author

Catherine—Kathryn—Sr. Bartholomew—Sr. Barty—Sr. Kathryn. By all these names the author of *God's Brat* has been known at different periods of time throughout her life.

Born in rural Northeastern Nebraska just a few years before the Great Depression, Kathryn Leahy followed the Lord's call to the Sisters of St. Francis in 1936 and, at age sixteen, went by train to their Mother House at Stella Niagara, New York. Two years of novitiate training introduced her to the ways of Religious Life. There she assumed the name Sr. Bartholomew.

After three years of training at a Normal School in Buffalo, New York, her first teaching assignment (1941) was at St. Agnes Academy in Alliance, Nebraska. Other teaching assignments took her to St. Elizabeth School, an inner city school, in Denver, Colorado; to St. Mary's School at Rushville, Nebraska; to St. Francis Mission at St. Francis, South Dakota and to St. Mary's Academy at O'Neill, Nebraska. During these teaching years, Sr. Barty completed classes for a B.A. Degree from St. Ambrose College in Davenport, Iowa (1945) and a M.A. Degree in education from Creighton University (1951). In addition to teaching, the years 1957–62 included administrative duties at Marycrest in Denver, Colorado—while a new Motherhouse was built and an all-girl Catholic high school was opened.

While in Rome, Italy studying Theology (1962–64), she witnessed the opening of Vatican II Council, was in St. Peter's square when Pope John XXIII died, and again to receive the first blessing of Pope Paul VI.

Different challenges came with her assignments to the Diocesan School Office in Grand Island, Nebraska (1967–72), and to a Black Community in Birmingham, Alabama (1972–74).

One more career change awaited her at Marycrest in Denver. Beginning in 1974, her work was in St. Mary Magdalene Parish as Pastoral Care Minister. This meant visiting the sick, the home-bound, nursing home residents, terminal patients in a cancer hospital, and weekly volunteer visits with women in Denver County Jail. She continued with this type of work until her retirement.

At the time of her Golden Jubilee celebration in 1988, many expressed their appreciation for her and her work. Excerpts from some of the congratulatory messages she received then are revealing:

"You are one God has chosen to bring peace and comfort to the sick and lonely. You gave me courage and strength ....."

"We all love her. She is wonderfully sensitive to people; a caring, loving person, with a delightful sense of humor."

"No matter what race, color or creed one may be, she always takes the time to listen and offers a caring word."

"She's a golden ray of sunshine who comes with love and blessings and always brings me a treat."

"... became a great inspiration to me in prayer and in friendship."

"She has served beyond the call of duty."

"She has enhanced my spiritual life and lifted my spirits on many an occasion."

"She has lots of patience and she always has a joke."

"We are crazy about her."

One person summed up her work during that time, "Sister acted as God's Angel of Mercy." Even now, in retirement, she still shows high concern for others well being!

In the 1970s, Sister Kathryn Leahy discovered a passion for writing. Write, she did! And write, she does! Now one can only wonder, "What's next?"

Do take time to savor some of her works!

❖ ❖ ❖ ❖ ❖

Printed in the United States
81815LV00003B/1-105